"Pardon Me, But You're Eating My Doily!"

# "Pardon Me, But You're Eating My Doily!"

## Robert Morley

ST. MARTIN'S PRESS/NEW YORK

*Design by M. Paul*

Library of Congress Cataloging in Publication Data
Morley, Robert.
  "Pardon me, but you're eating my doily!"

  1. Anecdotes.  2. Wit and humor.  I. Title.
PZ6261.M78  1983      082      82-16983
ISBN 0-312-59656-1

First Edition
10 9 8 7 6 5 4 3 2 1

# Contents

# Preface

I do hope this little volume will be as much fun for the reader as it was for me to compile. Many people, most obviously the marvelous contributors, were of great help with the book, and my spirits were immeasurably lightened by the sheer fun which everyone took in recounting their favorite blunders and misadventures. All of us have had moments of acute embarrassment—forgetfulness, confusion, the deadly, misplaced modifier—that at the time made us want to bury our heads, nay, our entire bodies, in the nearest dune. It is cheering, therefore, to see how willing people have been to "tell all" in order to help a worthwhile charity.

All royalties for this book will be divided between the National Society for Autistic Children in both the United Kingdom and the United States. None of the contributors received a penny for their efforts, only the satisfaction of knowing they were helping children. Besides tales from writers, journalists, and a wide selection of other professionals, my simple note of appeal brought forth a splendid variety of gaffes from those *truly* professional performers: politicians and actors. I knew my colleagues in the acting profession could be counted on for some good anecdotes, but it was delightful to see how figures of all political stripes responded with wit and enthusiasm. So I am able to offer not only a good sampling from both the Lords and Commons, but also the stories of a former President, a sitting President and Vice President, the Speaker of the House, the Senate Majority Leader, and others.

It seems only fair that since the American royalty is included, I should—even at second hand—add a few anecdotes involving the British First Family. Now that the heir apparent has become both husband and father, I hope it will be perhaps permissible to start with a delightful collection of royal boo-boos generously provided by my friend Hugo Vickers.

Mr. Vickers instances a number of *faux pas* by the late Duke of Windsor. In his early youth, travelling in the royal train, through Tasmania, he espied in his drawing room an indicator revealing the speed at which he was travelling. The dial registered eleven miles an hour. "Bloody nonsense," he is reported to have observed. "They might at least have seen that this was working properly." And, adjusting what he believed to be the regulator, he inadvertently applied the vacuum brake. The train came to an unscheduled stop and the timetable for the day was considerably disorganized, especially as His Royal Highness was loathe to take responsibility for what had occurred.

In New Zealand, H.R.H. was credited with knighting the wrong man, while in Fiji he opened a ball at Government House by claiming as a partner the lady typist of the chief Indian agitator on the island. In Melbourne, when the Prime Minister pointed out his son in a far corner of the room, the Prince went happily to where two men stood and shook hands with the one in evening dress only to discover that he was a waiter. At another dinner party in Australia the guests were invited to close their eyes and draw pigs on the menu. The Prince of

Wales turned to his hostess and heard himself saying, "I shall look at you and get my inspiration."

Prince Edward's brother, the Duke of Gloucester, Mr. Vickers reminds us, was not exactly a dab at light conversation. On one occasion, after witnessing a display of belly-dancing in Cairo, he was subsequently introduced to the performer. They sat in silence for several minutes before the Duke inquired, "Do you know Tideworth?"

There are few instances of the present Queen ever being disconcerted or put out by the inane remarks made to her by her subjects, although, when Robert Graves went to Buckingham Palace to receive a gold medal for poetry, the Queen told him it was the first time she had presented such a medal. "Congratulations, Ma'am," replied Graves, after which the audience terminated rather abruptly. But I prefer to think that Her Majesty had a busy day in front of her—possibly a royal garden party.

It was on one of these occasions that I—flushed at the success of my riposte to Prince Charles, who had inquired what on earth I was doing there: "The same reason as yourself, sir," I replied. "It's good for business."—then found myself conducting the late Prince Chula of Siam to a chair as I explained that this was an admirable vantage point to observe Her Majesty actually sipping the Earl Grey. The Prince shook me warmly by the hand, stepped over the ropes, and made his way to the royal tea tent where he stood for some time munching an eclair and making conversation with the monarch.

Finally, as we step off the royal carpet, I am indebted to Mr. Vickers for his delightful account of a dinner party presided over by Sylvia Brooke, the daughter of Lord Esher. She was newly married to the last white Rajah of Sarawak. A lull in the conversation occurred, but, to her relief, she was able to announce to her guests, "Listen, it's started to rain at last." The guests remained dumb in silent horror as the young Ranee turned to see the old Rajah blithely relieving himself over the veranda.

Which reminds me of a tale still told at the Melbourne Club of an elderly grazier who, unwilling to trust his bladder another second, seized the sugar bowl, emptied out its contents, and hastily transferred it to his lap. Alas, the sugar bowl was inadequate, and for some minutes his guests were treated to the sound of rushing water. It became a favorite joke at the club for irreverent strangers to test the sugar for moisture and, on one occasion at least, to demand "one of your dual-purpose tankards."

I leave it to Andrew Sinclair to provide, in this volume, yet another gem of this genre. If we were giving prizes again this time, I would award it to a lady who prefers to remain anonymous. As a young girl, she was introduced at a party to a blind man, whom she found successfully maneuvering his teacup. Temporarily at a loss for conversation, she made an extravagant play for another guest's dog, petting the creature enthusiastically until the blind man inquired, "Is that a dog you're talking to?"

"Yes," she told him.

"Do you like dogs?" was the next question.

"Very much," she said.

"Have you got a dog?"

"We did have a dog, but he went blind and we thought it kinder to put him down."

Oh my.

Lest I go on and start giving away the treasures which follow, I will conclude with thanks again to all the wonderful contributors. And finally, my deep gratitude is due to you, gentle purchaser, for helping an autistic child. I hope you enjoy our effort on their behalf.

"Pardon Me, But You're Eating My Doily!"

# Dannie Abse

## DOCTOR AND POET

That particular Friday, because I was going to spend the weekend in South Wales, I hoped to leave work early, but the relief radiographer proved to be incompetent and slow. All the X rays sent to me were either underdeveloped or overdeveloped, underpenetrated or overpenetrated, or partially fogged. Patient after patient had to be returned to the X-ray department for a repeat X ray.

At last it seemed that there were no more X rays for me to read and it was time to leave. I would catch a later train from Paddington than I had intended. I was at the door when the telephone on my desk again rang insistently; it was the inept radiographer.

"Could you hang on, sir?" he said. "There's one more patient. Dr. Wicks would like you to report on it now. When it's ready, I'll bring the X ray to you."

I can't remember exactly how I responded; I suppose I gracelessly said something like, "All right, but don't bugger up the film this time." I returned to my desk and to pass the time read the current *British Medical Journal.* Then I looked at my watch. I had missed another train, and now half an hour had passed since the radiographer had called me.

I was halfway through a paper on *"Pseudomyxoma Peritonei:* An Unusual Case" when I decided that enough was enough and I stamped out of the room towards the X-ray department, where I at once encountered the radiographer emerging from the darkroom. "It's just developed, Doctor," he said before I could say a word. "Will you read it wet?"

In the darkroom there is a screen on which wet

X-ray films can be hung. The radiographer placed the film on it and turned a switch so that the screen lit up brilliantly behind the X ray. I looked at it astonished. The posterior-anterior view of the patient's chest—the usual view—was at an extraordinary tilted angle of forty-five degrees: the left shoulder was way up, the right shoulder way down. I had never seen anything like it.

Sarcastically I tilted my head at an angle of forty-five degrees as I scrutinized it and said tightly, "How the hell did you manage that?"

"Well . . ." he said.

"For God's sake," I roared, "all day you've messed things up and now this is utterly skew-whiff."

"The patient's behind you, sir," the radiographer urgently interrupted me.

I turned from him towards the open darkroom door, put on a suitable smile, and approached the patient in order to reassure him.

"Your X ray is normal," I said. "It's fine, though it's tilted somewhat. The radiographer has somehow cleverly contrived to make you look like a cripple. That's what I was complaining to him about. Don't *you* worry."

"Can I go now?" asked the patient.

"Of course," I said, smiling benignly.

And the patient, unsmiling, rose, one-legged, to limp pronouncedly over the brown linoleum of the X-ray department and through the door to disappear from my sight, but never entirely from my mind. I turned to the radiographer who lounged, rather than stood, against the wall, his face a study of sweet magnificent triumph.

# Brian Aldiss
**SCIENCE-FICTION AUTHOR**

In the 1970s I was a guest at a large conference at Poznan in Poland. To give you an idea of how important it was, we were blessed by the presence of a live Russian cosmonaut—the Eastern bloc's equivalent of having the Pope to open the Birmingham Motor Show. I was the only English guest, but there were large delegations from all the Eastern European states.

The official proceedings were deadly dull, but the "après-ski," as so often happens, was fun. In particular, I found myself the recipient of much hospitality from the Bulgarian group. This was before Bulgarian Technology had invented the Death Umbrella, and all was comradeship. Of course, Bulgarian national habits differ from ours: they drink fermented mares' milk, put their surname before their given names, and smoke a lot of cigarettes without incurring any Government Health Warnings. I also observed on that occasion that they have a wide variety of drinks—*kvass* apart—unknown in the West. I investigated that phenomenon whilst they plied me with questions about science fiction. In particular, they wanted to know a great deal about *Brave New World.* It so happened that I had boned up on that novel recently and was, therefore, able to respond rather fully, squeezing my replies through the language barrier and waiting patiently, glass in hand, whilst the interpreter of the group translated what I said to the others. This took place in their suite. Rarely have I had a more attentive audience.

I told them what I saw as the sterling virtues of

the novel, also pointing out a few seeming flaws. When we got to the flaws, some of them protested rather politely, somewhat in the matter of Canute, who bidst the mighty oceans deep their own appointed limits keep, without expecting much by way of response.

Finally, they had had enough and said, "Mr. Aldous, you have been very frank about your wonderful novel, and we thank you so much. You have been marvellously modest about it."

# Steve Allen

**COMEDIAN**

Two memorable moments of embarrassment occurred years ago, when I was still married to my first wife, Dorothy. One evening we were lying in bed, and it suddenly occurred to me that I would greatly enjoy eating a nice, cold, ripe persimmon that I had earlier in the day placed in the refrigerator. So, moving with the precision and grace of Stan Laurel in a silent movie, I walked to the kitchen, removed a saucer from the cupboard, took the squishy persimmon out of the icebox, placed it on the saucer, walked back into the bedroom, placed the saucer-with-persimmon on the bed, went over to the wall to turn off the ceiling light, came back to bed, and, forgetting where I had placed the persimmon, simply lay down on top of it.

The next two hours were spent trying to get persimmon juice off my back, my pajamas, the sheets, the mattress, the blankets, Dorothy, the rugs, the ceiling, etc.

The other thing was—if possible—even dumber than that. It happened during the rush of Christmas week when I was a bit on the punchy side from working long hours, Christmas shopping, etc. I was a few days late in setting up a Christmas tree for the children, so I raced over to a lot on Lincoln Boulevard, selected a suitable tree and placed it on top of my car to take home. Only at that point did it occur to me that I had forgotten to bring rope to tie the tree on. But traffic in the neighborhood was light, and, inasmuch as our house was only a few blocks away, I thought that by steering the car with one hand and reaching out the window to hold the tree with my left hand, I could get away with it. I thereupon sat myself in the car—with the door open, naturally—reached up with my left hand, got a good firm grip on the tree trunk, and then, with my right hand, reached out and closed the door very vigorously. If you try that sometime, you will make the interesting discovery that the upper part of the door mashes the hell out of your arm.

# Edward Asner

**ACTOR**

In New York in the late fifties, I fell asleep offstage during the second act of *The Three-Penny Opera.* I was startled awake to make my entrance and, in trying to stand and finish costuming myself, found my entire leg asleep—from hip to toe. My heart was pounding, as it does when being suddenly awakened, and the pain from my sleeping leg left me dragging along by my arms, attempting to get down the stairs and make my entrance.

Finally, I delivered my first two lines from off-stage at the top of the stairs, hoping to give my actor *on* stage the ability to stall for time. From my darkness on the stairs I heard, "Forget it, Ed—it's too late." The curtain came down, completely omitting the second-act finale of *The Three-Penny Opera.*

As the third act opened, I found myself in the presence of the most confused audience I ever saw.

# Michael Aspel

**BROADCASTER**

I was once, and only once, invited to a reception at the Iranian Embassy. A well-meaning colleague at the BBC provided me with what he described as an all-purpose greeting in Farsi, which I learned by heart. When I was introduced to the Ambassador, a large, hairy man, I recited the phrase perfectly. He gave me a wintry smile and moved away. An interpreter explained that I had just told the Ambassador that I would not exchange the moles on his cheeks for all the riches in Samarkand and Bokhara. No wonder the poor fellow looked puzzled: His Excellency was wondering, no doubt, who had told me about them.

# Gene Autry

## "THE SINGING COWBOY"

Although I have had my share of "embarrassing" moments when I was active as a performer, I think often of an incident which occurred when I was making personal appearances in England way back in 1939.

I was appearing at the Paramount Theatre in London, and we were fortunate to be playing to sell-out crowds. This particular time, as I was nearing the end of my performance, Bill Saul, who was the press agent for Republic Pictures, came backstage and said, "Gene, you won't believe the crowd that has gathered outside waiting for you to come out after the show—must be a few thousand people out there. I'd like to get some publicity shots of this, so instead of leaving by the stage door tonight, I want you to come down the center aisle when you finish your final number and exit the front of the theatre. I'll have two or three cameramen out there so we can get the best possible coverage of the crowd."

Well, I did as he asked, but as soon as I walked out I felt as though I had been hit by a tidal wave—the fans just converged on me and I couldn't even move. Bill had stationed himself and one of the photographers on the hood and roof of a car that had been left parked in front of the theatre, and I could hear him yelling at me to head his way. I finally managed to get to the car, and he leaned over and said, "Give me your hand and I'll help you up here." I vaulted onto the roof of the car, and just as I made it, the entire top of the car gave way to our weight and all three of us were unceremoniously dumped into one embarrassing heap in the middle of the car. A bobby came over to help untangle the mess and said to Bill, "Sir, is this your car?" He replied, "Oh, sure it is," and then we got out of there as quickly as we could. Luckily no one was hurt, and the only thing that suffered was my vanity. The thought of how we must have looked trying to extricate ourselves from that car still gives me a chuckle.

# Joan Baez

**SINGER AND ACTIVIST**

It happened a long time ago, but the years haven't lessened the embarrassment. While changing clothes for seventh-grade gym class, the bits of Kleenex which I had stuffed in my size-AAA bra fell out. There were plenty of amused witnesses, and I still remember that ghastly moment.

# Howard Baker
**UNITED STATES SENATOR**

My grandmother, a delightful lady who not long ago celebrated her 101st birthday, once served as the sheriff of Roane County, Tennessee. At a birthday party in her honor, Mother Ladd, as she is called, and I had the opportunity to chat with each other for a few minutes. Coincidentally, the party occurred just prior to my announcement as a candidate for President.

As we sat chatting, Mother Ladd looked inquisitively at me and asked: "Howard, are you really serious about this business of running for President?" I said I certainly was, to which she replied: "Well, OK then, I guess I'll support you." I told Mother Ladd I would certainly appreciate it. And she responded: "Look, Howard, I'm gonna support you. But I'll tell you right now, if you really want to go where the power is, run for sheriff!"

# Lucille Ball

**ACTRESS**

One of my most embarrassing moments was when years ago I had to audition for David Selznick's Scarlett O'Hara for the picture *Gone With the Wind.* I was so nervous and panicky, my knees gave out and I could not stand. I tried to beg off, but Mr. Selznick said, "OK, do the three scenes on your knees"—which I did. I did not get the part.

# Michael Bartman

BRITISH MARKETING DIRECTOR

It was a cold, rainy night and I was passing a friendly fish-and-chip shop when my wife and two children decided they would like to grab a bite to take home. The shop was in a busy road, and I parked on the opposite side of the street and suggested they might like to stroll across in the rain and pick it up for themselves. However, as they all refused, I reluctantly negotiated the traffic and joined the queue and, some fifteen minutes later, found myself at the head of it, to receive four soggy bags of fish-and-chips. I dashed across the road, threw myself into the driving seat, flinging the greasy parcels at my wife beside me in the passenger seat, and, muttering words of abuse, insisted that in future if the family wanted fish-and-chips they should bloody well go and fetch it themselves. My wife unaccountably started to scream, only it wasn't she but a total stranger! I looked up and through the windscreen to see my family in the identical car in front, making strong come-hither movements.

"Where's the fish?" was their only comment when I rejoined them.

# Kemp Battle

**NOTED RACONTEUR**

The scene is still vivid, though now long past. My stepfather held a government position and he and my mother were entertaining Prince (now King) Juan Carlos of Spain and his lovely bride. Upstairs, in the large sitting room near my bedroom sat the entire personal staff of the Prince and Princess waiting out the festivities on the floor below. I was thirteen, and their self-appointed host and entertainer. Grunting monosyllables and making elaborate gestures, I tried to explain to them simple things in English—like what baseball was, and how to make a peanut butter sandwich. They sat attentively, their faces turned up toward me in good will and eager anticipation. I made no headway; there was not a moment when either I or my polite listeners could truly say that we understood one word the other was saying. I became frustrated and at one point, staring at a smiling face, I said, "You don't know what I am saying, do you?" The face was happy and there wasn't a trace of "no" in those anxious, well-meaning eyes. "Is it because you are dumb?" I said brightly, nodding "yes." To my delight, the head rocked in rhythm with my own and said, "Si, si." The idea that I could say anything aloud that I wanted to—with no consequence— dawned on me with the sweetest pleasure. "And you," I said to one of the plump attendants of the Princess. "You are like a cow, aren't you?" and I whispered "moo," whereupon the group echoed me with the Spanish word for cow.

There was great celebration as we discovered the new game—I provided the noise and they would joyfully shout the Spanish equivalent. It was my own private pleasure that along with each animal's sound came the insult of comparison. "This one here looks like a monkey," I whooped, and swung on imaginary vines, doing what I thought was a perfect rendering of the face of the Prince's valet. Again, the group answered with happy cries of "monkey, monkey." I went through the room, calling out animals of all kinds, each comparison less flattering than the last. I was heady with power—the miracle of language, I suppose. I could say any insult that came to mind and I did.

The loveliest of the servants, a beautiful young woman who was the Princess's personal maid, seemed to enjoy the show most of all. I was drawn to a finale at her feet. I bowed before her, and though I cannot here repeat what I said, it had something to do with jungle nakedness and caves. She smiled on and on, and I, now drunk with arrogance, turned to the whole room and said, "Except for this broad, you are all pigs!" and there was the snorting sound and the chorus of "pig, pig" in Spanish.

It was a fitting conclusion to my night of insults. Debasing people had made me tired and to my audience's disappointment I went to bed. However, I was to see them all one last time, leaving through the receiving line at a party that my stepfather and mother held the following day. All the animals passed through, after which the Prince and Princess and my lovely junglewoman brought up the rear. I stood by my mother's side, hair neatly combed, the dutiful son, who, to everyone's delight, had practiced saying goodbye in Spanish. The young woman stopped in front of my mother and to my amazement, then horror, said in perfect English, "I must congratulate you on the talents of your son. He is quite good with foreigners." As my face reddened and my knees turned rubbery, my mother said proudly, "He has always wanted to work in the United Nations." (It was true.) The young woman turned, and looking directly at me, said evenly, "How charming. You must start right away with languages, don't you think?"

# Orson Bean

**ACTOR AND WRITER**

Some years ago my then wife, Carolyn, and I were vacationing at a resort in the Virgin Islands. At 2:00 A.M. on a hot night we found ourselves unable to sleep. Looking out the window of our beachfront cottage, we saw that all was dark and quiet; not a tourist was stirring. So we decided to go for a skinny-dip. By the light of the moon we ran, sans bathing suits, down the path some fifty yards to the balmy Caribbean water. There is a particular pleasure to swimming naked; we laughed and tumbled and hugged.

As we were about to climb out of the water and run back through the protecting darkness to our cabin, the entire beach suddenly lit up. Or so it seemed to us. What in fact had happened was that the light on the porch of the cottage next to ours had been switched on. The occupant of that room, a businessman to whom we had nodded a few times in the hotel dining room, had, like his neighbors, apparently been unable to sleep. So he had come onto his front porch for a late-night read of his *New York Times.*

Out in the water we waited. And waited. And began to turn blue. The only way back to our cabin was past his cabin. There was no towel with which to cover ourselves, nor even so much as a palm leaf lying on the beach. The one rational choice became apparent. Standing up, I offered my arm to my wife. She took it, and together we leisurely climbed the beach to our room. As we walked past the businessman, he glanced up from his *New York Times* to see a naked man and woman strolling the path in front of him. "Good evening," we said. "Good evening," he answered, then quickly looked back down at his paper.

We managed not to laugh, but once inside and under a hot shower, we howled. And went to bed, but not to sleep. Embarrassment—thank you, Robert Morley—can be liberating.

# Sally Bell

In the summer of 1966, when we were travelling on the ferry from Brindisi to Patras, I was standing patiently in a queue (very British) for coffee when Robert Morley's voice boomed from the back and over our heads—in Greek—asking for two coffees. In a flash he was served. I had to wait another ten frustrating minutes. If I'd had a brick I would have dropped it in his coffee!

ΔΕΝ ΦΤΕΩ ΕΓΩ ΑΝ ΔΕΝ ΜΙΛΑΣ ΤΗΝ ΓΛΩΣ-ΣΑΝ ΚΥΡΙΑ. ΕΣ ΑΛΛΟΥ ΕΚΕΙΝΕΣ ΤΙΣ ΜΕΡΕΣ ΣΥΧΝΑ ΜΕ ΣΥΝΧΗΖΑΝ ΜΕ ΤΟΝ ΜΑΚΑΡ-ΙΤΗΝ ΚΥΡΙΟΝ ΟΝΑΣΗ.

# Leonard P. Belson

**OPTICIAN**

Every optician spends a considerable amount of his professional life adjusting spectacles which, through normal wear, have become loose or uncomfortable. We become quite used to hearing tales of woe from our patients who have sat on their spectacles, lost their screws, or are suffering from broken "arms" and "legs." But the demure little old lady who confronted me this time was completely original.

"Can you tighten me specs, luv?" she asked. "They drops orf every time I goes to the toilet."

My waiting room, crowded with patients, suddenly came alive. Magazines with the latest news of the *Titanic* and eyewitness reports of the crash of the R.101 were put down, and all heads swivelled round at this unheard-of phenomenon. I knew instinctively that I should not ask the inevitable question, but curiosity got the better of me.

"How can your spectacles fall off when you go to the toilet?" I asked.

I was treated to the type of withering look reserved for the imbecile as she bent down to illustrate her reply: "Simple, luv. When I bends dahn to pick up me knickers, they falls orf!"

# Tony Benn

## MEMBER OF PARLIAMENT

This true story concerns the late Percy Wells, who
was the MP for Faversham in Kent. His last train
from Victoria Station ran at about 10:30 P.M., and
therefore he was always anxious that he might miss
it when we had a division at the end of the Commons
debate at 10:00 P.M.

As a result, he used to push himself to the front
of Members queueing up in the Division Lobby, and
as soon as the doors opened, he would rush through
and, having been counted in the Division, would
dash downstairs and get a bus to Victoria Station to
catch his train.

We all knew this, and so we used to make way
for Percy to push to the head of the queue night after
night.

One night Percy brought his wife to dinner at
the House, and after dinner they were sitting having
a cup of coffee when the Division Bell rang for the
ten o'clock vote. Percy went upstairs into the Division Lobby, where colleagues pushed him to the
front as usual, and then he rushed off to Victoria
Station, where he caught the last train. But when he
got home, the lights were out and the house was
locked, and he realized that he had left his wife
sitting in the House of Commons. She presumably
discovered what had happened after an hour or two
and was obliged to spend the night in a hotel in
London.

This story went round the House of Commons
very quickly, and ever after that, whenever there
was a late vote, people used to make way for Percy

and push him to the front, but they would always tap him on the shoulder and say, "Have you got your wife with you, Percy?"

Percy was a charming, modest man, and this story used to amuse and embarrass him at one and the same time.

# Michael Bentine

**COMEDIAN AND WRITER**

I was at an audition. There was a woman singing on the stage; her voice was so awful that I turned to the man sitting beside me and remarked upon it. He replied very frostily, "That is my wife." Pink with confusion, I hastily stammered, "I didn't mean her voice was awful, only the song she was singing." To which he replied, "I wrote it." I slunk away.

# Erma Bombeck

**WRITER**

I have made a career out of exploiting humor at my own expense. There is one incident I would like to forget, but somehow it keeps surfacing.

It has to do with the fifth anniversary of *Good Morning, America.* The entire "family" had been invited to New York to appear live on the show and do what we do best. At the end of the show, David Hartman looked into the camera and said, "We only have a minute left. What better time to hear from our resident humorist, Erma Bombeck?" The red light of the camera zoomed over at the resident humorist, who stood there and to thirty million people said, "Huh?" Somehow "huh" never filled in sixty seconds as I hoped it would.

# *Victor Borge*

**ENTERTAINER**

As Chairman of CARE's International Public Service Committee, I was at the White House to present a token of appreciation from the organization to President Lyndon Johnson for his support of CARE. It was at the height of the Vietnam conflict, and I recall that everything surrounding the ceremony was hurried and impromptu. The President rushed into the Oval Office from meetings with top advisers; we shook hands; he pushed a button, and into the room came a flood of TV cameras, photographers, and news reporters. Following my brief words of commendation for the President's efforts, in accepting his award Mr. Johnson said, "Yes, none of us can do enough for this worthy cause." And I responded, "Indeed, Mr. President, you have certainly proven that." I couldn't understand then why the President had such a surprised look on his face.

# Mel Brooks

ACTOR AND DIRECTOR

I was waiting outside a popular restaurant in Hollywood, shielding my face discreetly so I would not be recognized by out-of-towners seeking autographs. My ploy obviously failed because a short, bald man rushed at me with a pleading look in his eyes and said, "I hate to annoy you, but could you please . . ." I shouted back at him, "All right, all right. Quick, get me a piece of paper." Without a second's hesitation, he rushed off and rushed back triumphantly with a piece of paper in his hand. I then yelled, "A pen, you fool, a pen." In a panic, he searched himself to no avail. He rushed into the restaurant and immediately returned, waving the pen which he dutifully gave to me. I then said, "All right, all right, what's your first name?" He looked puzzled for the briefest moment and then blurted out, "Don." I said, "Good, good, all right, Don," and then I wrote as I always do, on the piece of paper, *To Don, All the best, Mel Brooks,* signed it with a flourish, and handed it to him with a sigh of relief. He took the paper, hesitated, and then said, "This is very good of you, but what I really wanted was some change to make a telephone call." It was the most embarrassing moment of my life, saved only by Don's wife, who looked at the paper as they left and shouted back, "Thank you, Dr. Blanc."

# Dr. Joyce Brothers
**PSYCHOLOGIST**

Several years ago, I was introduced on a talk show and came out onstage. Another guest, Rosie Greer, an enormous American football player, was standing directly in the way of my seat. As I attempted to circle him, I miscalculated the distance (it was greater than I had anticipated) and fell flat onto my rear end. This was probably the most undignified entrance ever made on a talk show.

# Art Buchwald

**COLUMNIST**

Robert Morley, once again, has leaned very heavily on me to tell of some embarrassing moment or instance of forgetfulness. My problem is that I always forget such instances.

I do recall one, and it had to do with Princess Grace and Prince Rainier. I was covering their wedding for the European edition of the *New York Herald Tribune.* The wedding took place on the eighteenth of April, and it was a magnificent event. I couldn't wait to call my wife and tell her about all the details. I thought she would be very pleased that one of us had made it into royal circles. To my surprise, after an elaborate description all I got from her was a frosty "very nice." I thought she was angry because I was living it up and she had to give baths to our three children.

Two days later it all became clear. I had forgotten her birthday. It was, however, the last time I did because now every year when I send an anniversary card to Princess Grace and Prince Rainier, I also buy a birthday card for my wife.

# George Burns
**ACTOR AND COMEDIAN**

I did an act years ago called Brown & Williams, Singers, Dancers and Smart Patter, at the Savoy Theatre on Thirty-Fourth Street. At one performance my fly was open, and the audience kept laughing, although I didn't know why. For the second performance I remembered to button my fly. No laughs. So the manager came back and told me to open my fly for the third show. That's when I was embarrassed.

# Leo F. Buscaglia

**AUTHOR**

Anyone who has ever seen me work on a lecture stage, television show, or whatever knows that I have a tendency to lose myself and become intensely involved in my presentation. The physiological result of my total involvement is a profusion of perspiration. It pours from my body, down my back, over my forehead, into my eyes, and I emerge looking as if I've just run a hundred-yard dash on a summer day in Bangkok.

To assure myself some appearance of propriety, I never go out for a lecture without at least three or four neatly pressed white linen handkerchiefs which I have folded in my trouser pockets. As I use each, I discard it temporarily on the podium before me and reach for another.

I was recently recording a television program before a large audience. I was well into the material and had already discarded two handkerchiefs. Without out a break in continuity, I reached for number three, and proceeded to wipe my forehead and eyes—only to find to my horror that what I had taken for a handkerchief was, in reality, a pair of pressed white briefs—underwear which had inadvertently been piled among the laundered handkerchiefs.

With as much poise as I could muster under the circumstances, I completed the dabbing and quickly returned the underwear to my pocket.

I often wonder how many viewers in the national audience shared the "brief" embarrassment.

# George Bush

VICE-PRESIDENT OF THE UNITED STATES

Having raised five children, there are many memories I cherish, and some I would rather forget. One incident in particular was the time a good friend and neighbor casually mentioned how enterprising our young son was. He apparently felt his allowance was quite inadequate and, much to our chagrin, was selling a well-known cleaning product to all our neighbors, pointing out how many dirty things in their homes it would clean. My neighbor really didn't mind buying the product but wondered if I knew that the congressional license plates on my car were bordered with bumper stickers which read, "I Like Swipe!" Needless to say, we raised his allowance and discouraged further business ventures without first getting our approval.

# Jimmy Carter
**FORMER PRESIDENT OF THE UNITED STATES**

As a boy, my ambition was to go to the U.S. Naval Academy and become an officer in the Navy. Perhaps because of this, one of my heroes was Captain Horatio Hornblower, the famous character in C. S. Forester's novels about the Napoleonic wars.

Much later in my life, I was accepting for the second time my party's nomination for President of the United States—at the Democratic National Convention, assembled in Madison Square Garden in New York. One of my key paragraphs was designed to pay my respects to one of America's own great heroes, Senator Hubert Humphrey. I led up to the punch line, "... that great American, Hubert Horatio Humphrey!"—but instead, with more than sixty million television viewers in the audience, I said, "... Hubert Horatio Hornblower!"

# Diane Cilento

**ACTRESS**

I was returning from Australia to Italy, just after I had produced my first child. At the time my daughter was about five weeks old, and I was carrying her in the usual wicker basket and was armed with mounds of diapers, booties, and bonnets. We had already been travelling for many hours from Sydney to Darwin, to Singapore, and then to an unscheduled stop, Bangkok.

I was anxious to take advantage of this unexpected stroke of luck, as I had heard that the Thai carvings, jewelry, and paintings were beautiful, cheap, and unobtainable anywhere else.

Having left my basketload of baby in the hands of two enchanting ladies of the Mother's Room at the airport, I hurried off to examine all the tempting goods displayed in the stores. After an energetic and invigorating bout of bargaining, I became the proud possessor of a set of Siamese knives and forks carved with dancing figures, a large roll of Thai silk of varying purple hues, and a poster of some Thai boxers hurling themselves into the air at each other.

I rushed back to the airport clutching my booty in my arms and was hurried aboard the plane, as the last flight call had been made some time earlier. The engines roared, sweets were passed around, and I settled comfortably into my seat, contemplating with pleasure the surprise with which my delightful presents would be greeted. The great plane moved out on the runway.

As the roar of the engines gained momentum, I noticed that the chief steward and an air hostess were whispering to each other, peering down the cabin past me, frowning and gesticulating as another hostess joined them and whispered urgently into the ear of the worried steward. It was quite clear that something was up. I wondered vaguely if we had a terrorist on board.

The sound of the great engines decreased. I glanced out of the window, and in one blinding, heart-in-mouth moment the whole mystery was revealed: rushing down the runway were two lovely old Thai ladies carrying a basket between them which they lifted up momentarily for inspection. They were shouting, but I couldn't hear a word.

The body blush stayed with me for a good twenty-four hours; the disbelief and condemnation in the eyes of my horrified fellow passengers made the remainder of my journey quite memorable. But there is no use denying anything: I just totally and utterly forgot that I was no longer a footloose and fancy-free woman whose oyster was the world. Listen, it could happen to anyone. . . .

# Craig Claiborne

**FOOD EDITOR AND GOURMET**

As food editor of *The New York Times* and long before I assumed that position, I had a keen interest in dining around the world. During World War II, my knowledge of food was extremely limited and my travels even more so, although I was in my early twenties, incredibly innocent and inexperienced on many counts.

During World War II I was an enlisted man in the United States Navy, stationed aboard a communications vessel known as the *Ancon,* an AGC-4, anchored at times in various coastal ports of southern England. We were at one point anchored in Portsmouth, and I went ashore with a fellow enlisted man named Anthony Reno. I had never dined on high tea, although I had heard of it for most of my life. I asked Tony if he would join me late one afternoon at a tearoom which we happened to pass, and he agreed. As we approached the entrance we noted a sign on the door which said, "No prams allowed." We turned and walked away, not knowing in all our American innocence if we were prams or not.

# Dick Clark
**TV PERSONALITY**

Years ago, one of my co-workers was felled by a heart attack and died at the Los Angeles airport. This tragic event occurred on a Friday afternoon. His immediate family was thousands of miles away. As was only appropriate, we handled the necessary arrangements over the weekend. The following week I received a phone call from the man's bereaved brother, who thanked me for our efforts. It was then I made one of the more unthinkable utterances of my life. The deceased man's brother said in effect, "Thanks so much for arranging the funeral." I responded, "It was a pleasure."

# Lord Clark

ART HISTORIAN AND AUTHOR

Although I have been elected to nine clubs and have paid the entrance fees, I have resigned from all but one simply because I have been too embarrassed to speak to any of the members. This is a ridiculous shortcoming, the more so as I am very fond of talking; but I am still unable to conquer it. My only recent effort to be clubbable confirmed my fears. A dinner was given in the St. James's Club for Oliver Chandos, who had been its chairman for many years and had just been made a Knight of the Garter. As he was an old friend of mine, I thought I ought to attend. I found myself among a group of members, none of whom I remembered having seen, who naturally did not address a word to me. After about ten minutes a man who looked like a naval officer, wearing a claret-coloured bow-tie, advanced toward me and said, "You're Sir Kenneth Clark."

I agreed.

"The Bart, of course," he said.

"No," I said, "I am not a baronet."

"But you must be," he said; "the other Sir Kenneth Clark is a fearful shit; everybody says so."

"Well, I'm afraid I'm the only one." I fear we both blushed.

# Tom Conti
**ACTOR**

Some years ago I went to meet the producer of a series called *The Explorers*. I was then taken to meet the director. In true British fashion, I didn't listen to the name, but his face was so familiar that I knew he was an actor turned director. We chatted amicably for half an hour or so. He knew my wife's name and that I had a daughter; I complimented him on having done his homework. The film was to be made in the Australian outback, and we talked of the inadvisability of taking families on the "shoot." I asked whether he was taking his wife with him and the ages of his children, etc., all the while struggling to think who was the owner of this so familiar face.

As I left the office the name came—along with a cold flush and a mild buzzing in the ears—Lord Snowdon. I showed nothing, of course, but made my customary exit, trying to open the door the wrong way, catching my belt on the handle, and trying to say a controlled "good-bye" before calmly walking into the tea trolley in the corridor.

I tried to "play back" the conversation. How many gaffes had I made? What ghastly questions might I have asked? What was the last thing I saw you in? Is your wife an actress?

# Lady Diana Cooper

**AUTHOR AND ACTRESS**

Not recognizing people can always be the cause of embarrassment. I'm always telling people grotesque stories—which turn out to be about themselves.

The other day, when thousands of us were celebrating Sir Robert Mayer's hundredth birthday at the Royal Festival Hall, five hundred of us repaired to a special room during the entr'acte. There I was, mooching around without an escort, when a nice little woman equally unescorted came to my side to ask me if I did not think it wonderful.

"Wonderful," I replied, "and isn't he marvellous?"

"Marvellous," she replied, and so we rippled on in praise offhandedly for several minutes—during which time I noticed the size, sparkle, and splendour of the diamonds round her throat.

The penny dropped. I bungled an arthritic "bob," saying, "Oh, Ma'am. Please, Ma'am. I'm so sorry, Ma'am—I didn't recognize you without your crown."

# Norman P. Coxall

In the 1960s, when London was swinging, the Beatles were at their peak, and Carnaby Street was the mecca of all the young trendies, it was very smart amongst the young set to go to "in" places such as bistros or bistrotheques (which is a bistro and discotheque combined). The society photographer Tom Hustler ran such a place in Maddox Street called Fanny's; it's probably still in existence today.

My friend and I booked a table and took along two girls we hoped to impress. We told the girls that we were involved in Music and Fashion and anything else we considered to be remotely trendy, and they were very impressed.

On reaching the bistro, we were shown to our table, and the waiter busied himself with menus and napkins.

"Is young Hustler in tonight?" my friend enquired.

"You mean Tom Hustler, the guy that owns this place?" said the waiter.

"Yes, of course I do," replied my friend. "We're great chums." This really impressed the girls.

"That's odd," said the waiter. "I'm Tom Hustler, and I've never seen you before in my life."

# Lord Delfont

**IMPRESARIO**

I've committed a few faux pas in my time . . . but how about a joke instead?

Joe, feeling unwell, went to his doctor for a checkup. After a thorough examination, the doctor pronounced that Joe had only a short time to live.

Shocked, the doomed man said, "Will the end come in months or years?"

"No," said the doctor, "in a matter of hours, and, if I were you, I'd go home to bed and make myself comfortable."

Joe did this, but, becoming nervous, he called his friend Mo and said, "I'm dying. Won't you come over and talk with me in my last hours?"

Mo did as he was asked, and, after some hours of reminiscing, he fell asleep. Joe immediately roused him and said, "Please, Mo, don't go to sleep now."

Mo rubbed his eyes and grumbled, "It's all right for you, but I've got to go to work in the morning."

# Joe DiMaggio
**BASEBALL PLAYER**

Sometime in the 1940s, I don't remember exactly when, we were playing Detroit at Yankee Stadium. We were battling Detroit for first place (something we seemed to be doing all the time in those days), and there was a capacity crowd at the park. Late in the game a routine fly ball was hit to me in center field. I followed it easily, was under it well before I had to be, and the ball landed squarely in my glove. Then, to my surprise, it popped right out and fell to the grass. I was pretty embarrassed. There were, after all, nearly 60,000 people watching. But these things sometimes happen, so I picked up the ball and threw it in. The next batter, in fact the very next pitch, was hit to the same exact spot. I didn't even have to move. Down came the ball into my glove, and again it popped out and fell to the field. I can still see it lying there in the grass at my feet.

I had the reputation of being a pretty fair fielder, but two dropped balls in a row! I can guarantee that if I could've hid behind a blade of grass out there in center field that day, I would've.

# Jeane Dixon

## ASTROLOGER

Several years ago, during one of my speaking tours, I visited a large city in Ohio, where I was scheduled for an autograph party at the town's major department store. This was an important event in that community, and there was considerable advance advertising of my forthcoming appearance.

Little did I know that the city still had on its books an ordinance from the early nineteenth century, strictly regulating "the practice of astrology" and requiring a license before anyone could engage in it.

In fact, one enterprising citizen took it upon herself to go to the sheriff's office and secure a warrant for my apprehension if I were to defy the city's ordinance by failing to get an astrology permit.

Blissfully unaware of all this fuss, I flew into town and rode to the store, where a large crowd had gathered, some wanting autographed books, some hoping for a personal prediction, and some merely curious. I do believe a great time was had by all. I know I certainly enjoyed it.

After I returned to the airport for the next leg of my flight, and as I was getting ready to board, a phalanx of newsmen and photographers surrounded me. Flashbulbs popped and questions flew. The up-shot of their inquiries was: Is the sheriff on his way here with the warrant? Are you going to escape in time?

It took a few minutes to discover what they were talking about and why there was such a commotion. Fortunately, just then it was time to board the plane. And so I did not find out if the sheriff really was on his way. However, I did read in the newspapers the next day that the warrant was outstanding for my arrest, and that made news around the world.

Needless to say, I could not have been more embarrassed. Just for a moment, I felt like the most wanted outlaw in America.

# William Douglas-Home

**PLAYWRIGHT**

In early youth, while sitting with the grown-ups at lunch, I remember hearing my elderly Aunt Margaret assuring a retired schoolmaster, who had asked her if the county she lived in in Wales was over-populated, that it was, in fact, "very sparsely copulated indeed."

# Margaret Drabble
**NOVELIST AND BIOGRAPHER**

How I welcome this opportunity to relive one of the nastiest moments of my life! It occurred when I was watching for the first time what I think is called a rough cut of the only film I ever wrote that ever got made. Naturally, I found my own story deeply moving and was weeping copiously by the end. However, I was not so far carried away as to forget that I was sitting next to the composer of the music, to whom I had just been introduced. Politely, I blew my nose, turned to him, and said, "I thought the music was wonderful." He looked surprised (or offended, I dare not recall) and said, "But I haven't written it yet." I think I went on to explain that I wasn't really very musical, that I was in fact tone-deaf, but I don't suppose it did much good.

# Harold Evans
FORMER EDITOR OF *THE TIMES* OF LONDON

I was with a party of fellow journalists and their wives at an eatery in the King's Road where they had a fiddler who came to the table to play love songs, and his attentions greatly embarrassed the wife of my friend. He thought he knew the best way to cope with the unspoken entreaties. He took a ten-pound note from his pocket, showed it to her, and then attempted to tip the man so that he would go away. To do this without disrupting the host's conversation and upsetting him by appearing not to like the entertainment, he folded the ten-pound note and then leaned over the back of his chair to put it into the pocket of the violinist.

He found it difficult to get the tenner into the flap of the pocket and pushed and pushed. What he could not see, but everybody else watched with astonishment, was that he was trying to push the tenner into an opening at the top of the violinist's fly. The harder he pushed, the more the violinist bent his body to escape what he thought were amorous hands. But the violinist played gallantly on.

# Serena Fass
**TRAVEL AGENT**

A friend of mine was driving along happily, minding his own business, when all of a sudden a woman driver came tearing round the corner in the opposite direction on the wrong side of the road. Passing him, she rolled down the window and shouted, "Pig." My friend, quite astonished by this insult, replied, "Silly old cow." On turning the corner, he drove straight into a herd of pigs.

# *Christina Foyle*

**BOOKSELLER**

In the 1930s, I spent a holiday in America and watched Duke Ellington perform to an enraptured audience.

Coming home on the ship, we met some rich Americans, who were very conscious of their wealth and importance. One of them said to me, "My, I am looking forward to seeing your country. Do you know, I am related to Duke Ellington?"

"Really?" I said. "We saw him perform with his band in New York, and he was wonderful."

"I said the Duke of Wellington," was the frosty reply.

# Lady Antonia Fraser
**BIOGRAPHER AND MYSTERY WRITER**

I have a particular fondness for literary bumbles, having started very promisingly in my teens by insisting on conducting a whole conversation on the assumption that a man called Tristram Shandy wrote a book called *Laurence Sterne.* In vain my interlocutor tried, tactfully, to put me right. I gamely battled on: "Ah, but Shandy's understanding of Sterne . . ." It might sound rather brilliant these days.

Two other literary flubs concern my great-uncle and aunt, Eddie and Beatrice Dunsany. Aunt Beatrice charmed me as a child with the story of the rich and romantic American Lady touring Europe—before the First World War, I imagine. She was enchanted with the Europeans—especially the titled ones. Overhearing a conversation about Machiavelli's *The Prince,* she contributed enthusiastically: "Oh, the dear Prince! We met last fall and I just fell in love with him. . . . "

Uncle Eddie Dunsany—a man of wonderful and terrifying aspect—casually referred to a book called *Peace and War* during a conversation about Tolstoy with Maurice Bowra (then a young don). For a while Maurice Bowra managed to keep the conversation going without mentioning the title at all, thus avoiding the twin perils of contradicting his host and compromising himself. Finally, trapped by the turn the talk had taken and deciding to go for politeness, he too alluded to *Peace and War.*

*"Peace and War! Peace and War!"* roared Uncle Eddie. "You mean *War and Peace."* And he retired, absolutely delighted with the low level of culture among young Oxford dons.

# *John Gardner*

Two of my most humiliating moments have a common link—small airplanes. To me they have been
nothing but trouble:

I. Man of the World
Some years back when I was teaching medieval
literature at Southern Illinois University, an artist
colleague was commissioned to design a large foun-
tain-and-pool complex for the courtyard of a new
bank in Memphis. He needed to see the physical
layout; so I assured him that I had the clout to wan-
gle the use of a small plane from the S.I.U. fleet. We
invited along a photographer for the ride.

At the university airport, I led our trio out on
the tarmac behind the student pilot. He stopped just
short of the Cessna 172 and gestured to an open
door. I bowed with some fanfare and jumped in.

I found myself in a tiny, dark baggage compart-
ment, clutching my bulging briefcase. Mortification
struck, and I deliberated over whether or not to stay
right there and pretend I always rode in the steerage.

It was extremely difficult to scramble out again
and get in the proper door. My friends were already
seated. The photographer was up front next to the
pilot, and my friend was looking out the window
humming a little tune.

He asked, "Where you been, Johnny? Pilot's
been looking all over for you."

"Oh, I always like to inspect the plane first, you
know."

He replied seriously, "Better safe than sorry."

53

## II. The Bombing of Breadloaf

Not too many years ago my wife and I separated. During the time it took to arrange a divorce, the issue of money added insult to injury. When the issue reached overwhelming status, I asked a lawyer-cousin of mine to take over the finances. That particular summer must have been a long, penurious one for Joan, for it inspired her to write and print up a series of anti-Gardner pamphlets and deliver them to the writers' workshop where I was lecturing for a ten-day period in August—Breadloaf, near Middlebury College, in Vermont.

During my last Saturday at the conference, I was walking to my cabin for a rest when I looked up and spied a small plane circling above the Breadloaf compound. Even though it appeared to be losing pieces of itself, I was tired enough to plod on toward my bed for a much-needed nap. My son and his girl friend arrived a few hours later, and I sensed strange air and distance between us. They kept asking how I was, and I kept telling them I was fine, just tired.

At lunch in the big dining hall, I felt a sudden surge of paranoia, as if people were viewing me in a new way, as if my forehead or the seat of my pants displayed embarrassing words too filthy to utter. I perceived levels of curiosity and pity in the actions of many of the people there. They tipped their heads to one side when they spoke to me. But I attributed my extreme sensitivity to the fact that as a writer I am always more aware of human feelings than most (ahem).

That night at the final party, I found myself melting in gin for the first time in months. I could hear people muttering my name and looking my way even more than usual. This time I attributed their attention to my extreme drunkenness, and I shuddered with vulnerability, the whisper of secrets furling around my head. At the last breakfast, friends shook my hand and said sad good-byes. I had been to Breadloaf many times, but I had never encountered this kind of treatment. I had never been treated with this odd combination of sorrow, compassion, disgust, and amusement. Not even when I had been in the hospital for ages with The Dread Disease. Always before, people had either loved me or hated me; none of this mixed emotional weirdness had ever been my lot in life.

For months I occasionally mused on the last two days at Breadloaf, wondering what had been going on. Then in New York I saw an old friend who was able to answer my questions. She told me this:

Joan had written up some imaginary interviews, an accurate financial report, and a miscellaneous compendium of dispatches which she decided would make good outside reading at Breadloaf, where there is a large gathering of important writers and serious students. She determined that the best way to get everyone's attention would be to drop them from the sky in written form, so that all of those in attendance could read what a scoundrel I was being to my wife and children.

One of our daughter's many admirers happened

to have a pilot's license. He and Joan had flown over the mountains, buzzed Breadloaf, and let loose bundles of her propaganda. The directors, always nervously alert to trouble, had gotten immediate word of the drop and had managed to confiscate most of the leaflets, but not before a few poets had read them and told a few other people. Under strict administrative orders not to discuss the incident, no one dared breathe a word to me for fear Breadloaf's gate would be closed forever to any who dared inform.

My friend, who knows our family history well, said that the writing was very clever and witty, "not mean at all." I realized that I would have been less humiliated by knowing at the time what was going on than by suffering all the stares and silent commiseration I had felt swirling around me. In fact, I might have turned the event into a grand lecture on "Life Imitates Art and Vice Versa," or "Threats to Freedom of the Press."

As it was, the directors who thought they were protecting me and their summer workshop missed a fine opportunity to add yet another Breadloaf legend to the annals of writers' conferences, and I lie sleepless some nights wondering what in the world the pamphlets said.

# Fred Graham

LEGAL CORRESPONDENT

My most stunningly embarrassing moment in television came shortly after I left *The New York Times* to join CBS News. I rushed into the studio from an assignment, just as Walter Cronkite was announcing my story from New York. Then, just before the red light came on, on my camera, the makeup lady rushed forward and plopped a compact in my hand. Just as I went on the air, I looked down at the compact and realized for the first time that I had been appearing on television each night before twenty million people wearing a face powder called "Gay Whisper."

One of my less-than-towering moments came when CBS News correspondent Bob Schieffer and I arrived at an exclusive private party at the 1976 Democratic National Convention, only to find that the building was full and invited guests were being turned away at the door. Schieffer led the way and was waved aside, but the doorkeeper stared at me with a look of recognition; it was clear to me that I was about to score a great personal coup over Schieffer, as I was about to be recognized just after he had been turned aside as a nobody. Indeed, the doorkeeper, obviously familiar with my prematurely gray hair, announced: "Let that man in—that's Howard K. Smith!" Chastened but thankful, I entered, bringing my unrecognized friend Schieffer with me.

# Irene Handl

**ACTRESS**

We were doing *Blithe Spirit,* a play which I adore, and
I was playing a part which I adore, Madame Arcati.
The company was in great form; the laughs had been
coming regularly right through the show. Only the
last act to go: I arrive at Charles Constandine's house
at the witching hour, fetchingly clad in Chinese
pyjamas, bowed down by assorted herbs and strings
of garlic, plus a deep sense of shame at my failure to
definitively dematerialize that teasing, obdurate
sprite Elvira.

I put my herbs down somewhere handy, in case
they are needed for last-ditch tactics, and am starting
on preliminary incantations when I become aware of
a sensation that cannot be but recognized throughout the civilized world: the unmistakable slither of
trousers falling down. Suavely, inexorably, my black
satin trousers slid down toward my ankles, where
they were firmly taken into custody by Madame
Arcati's cycle clips. I was left standing in my Chinese
jacket, my suspendered hose, and my private underwear—a single garment of silk and lace known to the
lingerie trade as "cami-knickers." Mine were red—
a beautiful cerise, which lights more brilliantly than
anything I know except tinned cherries.

The actor playing Charles's part exploded.
Gripped by the terrible clips, I shambled into what
I hoped would be the dimmest corner of the stage
and tried to effect repairs. No use: the divorced ends
of the waist-belt refused to be reunited, and I would
have to play the rest of the scene holding everything
up. Ostrichlike, I had my back to the house, so I

didn't know that a malign moonbeam was lighting my tinned cherries.

After that nothing seemed to matter, as the whole place went up in an explosion of laughter which could be heard out in the street and wasn't extinguished on either side of the curtain till long after it had finally come down.

# Sir Nicholas Henderson

**AMBASSADOR**

Before paying an official visit to a town in France, I was given the usual briefing about leading personalities so as to help make the *entente* as *cordiale* as possible. I was told that the Préfet's wife was pregnant and that the Mayor's wife was very ill. At my first meeting I expressed pleasure and congratulations over the happy family news I had heard; at my second I commiserated, saying that I hoped Madame's condition would soon be *rétablie,* a phrase I had mastered with pride.

It was only after both interlocutors had remarked upon the eccentricities of the British and the pleasure that they had had in experiencing it at first hand that I made enquiries and discovered that I had got them the wrong way round.

# James Herriot

## VET AND AUTHOR

My absentmindedness, though constant and long-standing, has usually manifested itself in trivial ways. Brushing my teeth with shaving cream and wondering why the new toothpaste tasted so foul and made me foam at the mouth. Stopping in the middle of a veterinary round and trying to think where the devil I was going. Forgetting to put my dog back into the car after a country walk and having to dash back to the spot where, showing more sense than his master, he would be patiently waiting. Enclosing letters in the wrong envelopes with wildly embarrassing results.

However, there are two incidents which, though not world-shaking, may have caused certain people to doubt my sanity.

The first was when my wife asked me to take the sitting-room clock to be repaired. With my two young children in the car, I drove into the market-place of our little town and, clock under arm, entered the shop. Only it wasn't the right shop, it was the butcher's. My children, who always delighted in their father's affliction, watched, giggling, as, with my thoughts far away, I stood staring into the butcher's eyes.

I had been a customer for a long time, and the good man smiled in anticipation as he twirled his cleaver in his hand and I clutched my clock. This went on for several very long seconds before I realized where I was. There is no doubt I should have calmly purchased a pound of sausages, but my return to the world was too sudden, the prospect of explanation too unthinkable. I merely nodded briefly and left.

The other man in our town who probably thinks I am unhinged is a Mr. Craythorne. Some years ago he was manager of Mead's grocer's shop, his children went to the same school as mine, and he and I knew each other quite intimately.

He was standing in the doorway of his shop one day when I passed, my brain, as usual, wrestling with some distant problem, my eyes staring into space.

I heard his voice: "Now then, Mr. Herriot," and turned a blank gaze on him.

Only fellow sufferers will understand that at that moment I had not the remotest idea who he was. To whom, I desperately cogitated, belonged this very familiar face? Then, as I floundered, I noticed the word "MEAD" in foot-high letters above the shop window.

"Good morning, Mead," I cried heartily, giving him a smile compounded of friendliness and relief.

I had gone only a few steps before I realized that my greeting had been not only impolite but somewhat arrogant. I turned back and addressed him again.

"Good morning, *Mr.* Mead," I said.

It was only when I had turned the corner of the street and come to the surface that it dawned on me, too late, that his name was Craythorne and the time was late afternoon.

# *Olwyn Holden*

One Easter Sunday morning my husband sneaked a caramel chocolate from our daughter's Easter egg. The next moment he was writhing in agony, the chocolate having impacted or trapped a nerve in a tooth. I rang the dentist, who offered to come down to his surgery in about one hour's time. I then rang the doctor, who said to come over to his house and collect two very powerful painkillers. I jumped in my car and drove the twenty minutes to his house, twenty minutes back, to find my husband practically passing out with pain. I rushed into the kitchen, poured a glass of water, and swallowed the tablets myself.

# Frankie Howerd

**BRITISH COMEDIAN**

Just before the last General Election, I was attending a Sunday luncheon party. I entered the room looking for a friendly face, when a man came forward and held out his hand. I thought to myself, "Good, somebody I recognize—Peter Saunders, the impresario who presented *The Mousetrap.*" So I said cheerily, "Hello, are you still running? Is business good?" And he replied, "I'll let you know soon." "Funny," I thought, "what a strange reply." It took me thirty seconds to realize that it was in fact Lord Carrington, who the following week became Foreign Secretary.

# Rock Hudson

**ACTOR**

Have you ever tried too hard? Don't. It can boomerang. It did with me.

Some years ago I attended a fund-raising banquet where President John F. Kennedy was the guest of honor. At each table an extra chair had been placed for the President to sit and chat informally with the guests. I was anxious—too anxious—to find something—anything—that might be of some interest to him. Then I remembered that his name was Fitzgerald and so was mine. We had both recently returned from Ireland. There it was, something in common to open the conversation. Now I could relax and enjoy my dinner. Eventually the President reached our table. He turned to me, and before I could open the conversation with my cleverly planned words he said, "Your name is Fitzgerald, too. And you've just returned from Ireland—right?"

# Glenda Jackson

**ACTRESS**

At about the age of fourteen I was sent to do the weekend shopping, taking my youngest sister, aged three, in her pram. I finished the shopping, returned home, and only then discovered that pram plus baby had been left behind. I was not actually beaten until pram and baby had been safely returned.

# Rona Jaffe
**WRITER**

When I was just graduated from college and on the circuit of looking for Mr. Right by dating a different man every night, or the same man as often as he called—even if I didn't like him, since that was evidently preferable to staying at home—it was inevitable that I found myself constantly making the same inane small talk and listening to the same from them. Since we didn't talk about real feelings for fear of being found less than perfect, the small talk often got positively minute. Also, one got a little amnesiac about whom one had been out with when—if it's Tuesday it must be Jimmy. One night I was so desperate for conversation I started telling a story about an awful evening I'd recently spent with "a real bore." My date's eyes filled with an alarmed look of déjà vu. I suddenly realized that I was telling him the story of my previous date with *him!*

# Barbara Kelly
**BRITISH TELEVISION PERSONALITY**

I do rather tend to put my foot in it. Recently at an ambassadorial cocktail party, I became like a beleaguered "dodgem" car, completely immobilized in the crush. Struggling to regain momentum and at least secure a canapé, I volunteered to no one in particular, "This is just like the Black Hole of Calcutta."

"Were you there?" enquired Mrs. Indira Gandhi delightedly.

# Michael Korda
**EDITOR AND AUTHOR**

I once wandered onto a sound stage at Shepperton. I was just a small boy and was dutifully walking my dog, aptly named Nuisance, and suddenly found myself behind David Niven in the middle of a scene my uncle Alex was shooting for *Bonnie Prince Charlie*. My uncle, who was squinting through the viewfinder, closed his eyes and said, "Oh, my God!" Then he thought for a moment and told me, "My boy, try to remember, as a Korda you are supposed to be behind the camera, not in front!"

# Cleo Laine

**SINGER**

Like lots of mothers with firstborns and first walks to the shops, I left my baby outside the butcher's and walked back home alone. Whilst preparing the tea, I experienced a strong feeling of loss, of something misplaced. When my mother came in to ask where young Stuart was, I didn't wait to reply but sprinted back to find him quite happy, still outside the family butcher's shop.

Our third child also suffered, but not in the same way. Moving to a new house necessitated a change of school for young Jacqueline, my daughter. I enrolled her at the village school and proudly took her on the first day. When she arrived home after school, we questioned her about what she'd done. She wasn't very forthcoming but, pressed further, said, "Well, it's a bit babyish for me." A little worried, we went to see the headmistress.

Talking through the problem, she took our Jackie's enrollment papers and said, "Let's see, she was born in 1964, so she *should* be in the infants, but as she seems so advanced we will . . . "

"What year did you say?" asked her father.

"In 1964," repeated the headmistress.

John looked at me knowingly and accusingly: "You made Jackie a year too young; she was born in 1963."

The headmistress quietly closed the folder: "I think someone should come back and have arithmetic lessons, don't you?"

# Joseph Laitin
**POLITICAL CONSULTANT**

The first week I worked in the White House as deputy press secretary to President Lyndon B. Johnson, one of his aides said the President wanted me in the Oval Office immediately. It was the first time the President of the United States had personally summoned me. Almost instantly, I was standing in front of his huge desk, and it dawned on me in a few seconds that he wasn't behind his desk or anywhere in the office. Glancing through the glass doors opening out to the patio, I spotted the President in the Rose Garden, kneeling on the grass and staring intently at one of his beagles. I moved into the garden within a few feet of the President and waited to be recognized or acknowledged. I wasn't even sure the President knew who I was. I waited a few seconds, then coughed to establish my presence, but he never looked up. He was anxiously examining the dog's face, which I then observed was dripping from nose and mouth with a disgusting salivalike substance.

Suddenly, without moving his gaze from the dog's face, the President addressed me for the first time: "Joe," he said, "what do you think I should do about my dog?"

"Sir," I said, in my first response to the President of the United States, "first thing I'd do is give him a Kleenex." President Johnson, without looking up, put his hand on the dog's rear, shoved him in my direction, and said: "Go get him. Go sic Joe."

My wife maintains this incident was the beginning of the end of my relationship with him, and she may be right.

# Ann Landers

**ADVICE COLUMNIST**

One evening I was dining in the home of a socially prominent couple who were actually friends of a friend. Twelve of us were seated around one of the most beautiful tables I had ever seen.

After the entrée plates were removed, the waiter placed before me a Baccarat dessert plate and what appeared to be a most unusual lacy coconut dessert. I immediately took my knife in my right hand, my fork in the left and proceeded to cut into the exotic concoction.

To my surprise I found it quite tough but kept cutting away. Just as I was putting the fork into my mouth, the gentleman on my right said, "Eppie, what in the world are you doing?"

I replied, "I am trying to cut this coconut dessert, but it is terribly difficult."

"Coconut dessert," he gasped. "My dear, that's the doily!"

By that time I had carved out a considerable chunk, and to my utter horror, other guests were staring at me in shocked disbelief.

I offered a lame apology to the hostess, who was completely charming. She never asked me back.

# Prudence Leith

**CATERER AND RESTAURATEUR**

I once had the marquee tent for someone's wedding party put up in the wrong garden—next door, in fact.

When I first started cooking for my living, I had an Abyssinian cat who used to watch me filleting salmon and making *gateaux* from the windowsill. One day the telephone rang: "Is that two-two-nine-oh-six-eight-four?"

"Yes."

"Is your name Benny?"

"No, but my cat's is."

"Well, what the hell is his name tag doing in my salad?"

But my favourite catering disaster is the true story of the couple who went to the Far East on holiday. They wanted, besides their own supper, something to give their poodle. Pointing to the dog, they made international eating signs. The waiter understood, picked up the poodle, and set off for the kitchen—only to return half an hour later with the roasted poodle on a platter.

# Robert Ludlum

**WRITER**

By and large, an author's face is not overly familiar to the public, although his name might be. Consequently when traveling, especially under hectic circumstances, I frequently invent a name if a seatmate asks me, and if pressed for an occupation I usually say: "I'm in pipe. From Akron."

Invariably this brings a blank look, a nod, and I return to my reading without having to go through the Oh-You're-*Him* syndrome.

Several months ago I boarded a plane, exhausted from a full day of an "author's tour," and fell into my seat wanting silence, a newspaper, and quite probably a drink. This last was emphasized by the fact that my seatmate, a florid-looking gentleman of fifty-plus (the past thirty-five, I suspect, spent in a wine vat), was in the twelfth stage of inebriation.

With his eyes involuntarily crossing and a symphony of hiccups emerging from his throat through pursing lips in his swaying head, he asked me what I did for a living.

I replied: "I'm in pipe. From Akron."

He said: "I'll be a shon of a blitch, sho am I!"

I spent the next two agonizing hours learning all about "greenfield," "conduits," "stress tolerances," and all manner of incomprehensible things through vapors deadly enough to neutralize a herd of mastodons.

Now I say I'm a mortician.

# Roger McGough
**POET**

Last November I was invited to give a poetry reading at Walton Jail. I was pretty nervous about facing a "captive" audience of young long-term prisoners, some of whom were in for life.

It was a filthy morning, cold, gray, and rainy, and I was led into the room after much unlocking and relocking of iron doors. I took off my raincoat, shook it, and said cheerfully, "Lord, it's terrible out —you're lucky to be inside."

# Sir Fitzroy MacLean

**AUTHOR**

Some thirty-odd years ago, as a very young and rather nervous Member of Parliament, I stayed a weekend with a prominent and influential constituent. His wife, also a pillar of the local establishment, had a fine head of red hair.

I have always been fascinated by the contents of other people's medicine cupboards. Combined with a strong urge to experiment, I have always held the possibly rather dangerous view that, whatever it does to other people, no medicament is likely to have any effect on me. That night in the medicine cupboard I found a large bottle labelled "peroxide." I had heard of "peroxide blondes," then much in vogue. My hair in those days was dark brown. "I bet," I said to myself, "this stuff doesn't make *me* go blond," and, rubbing several lavish handfuls into my hair, I went to bed.

When I woke up next morning and looked in the looking-glass, I found to my amazement that my hair had in fact turned bright red, exactly the same colour as that of my hostess, who, as she presided over the breakfast table, quite clearly viewed me with the wildest surmise. Since then I have been rather more careful—at any rate with peroxide.

# Magnus Magnusson

## BRITISH JOURNALIST AND BROADCASTER

I, of course, have never been embarrassed, but when I was at Oxford, a fellow undergraduate got himself engaged to a delightful undergraduette, a jewel of the county set in Wiltshire. She was the daughter of an Admiral; he was a totally unsuitable suitor (as he proved later by becoming a very successful journalist).

The betrothal was fiercely resisted by the girl's parents. But eventually they relented sufficiently to allow the young man to be invited for a country-house weekend. Everyone found it a difficult occasion, socially.

On the Saturday evening, Daddy had invited a lot of his seafaring cronies to dinner. Our hero found himself seated well below the salt, and not even next to his affianced.

The talk was all of seas and ships and sealing wax, and our hero found himself out of his depth. So, for solace, he applied himself all too diligently to the claret.

Then, from the far end of the table where Daddy was holding court, there wafted down a word he felt he could recognize. The old sea dogs were discussing "buttocks," which, for the benefit of the uninitiated, means in nautical jargon "the breadth of the ship astern from its tuck upwards."

Here at last was a chance for our hero to make his mark on the conversation. Leaning forward, he bellowed up the table: *"Buttocks!* Did you say *buttocks?* My future wife has a splendid pair!"

The marriage did not take place.

# Walter Matthau

**ACTOR**

When I was introduced to Eleanor Roosevelt, I was so nervous and so flustered that I said the first words that came to mind—"Pleased to meet you." That, sir, is the biggest gaffe I ever made. I was pleased to meet her, but to make such a casual remark was very embarrassing. I was then told by the introducer not to feel unduly bad; Mrs. Roosevelt probably didn't notice my gaffe as she was very hard of hearing.

# Yehudi Menuhin

## MUSICIAN

My wife agonizes over my infinite capacity for forgetting names and my equal skill in triumphantly
misappropriating them. Of the two habits, she
would appear to prefer the former, for at least, she
says desperately, she can be called upon like some
dematerialized telephone directory to furnish me
with the missing name. Whereas with the latter she
has, as it were, hastily to erase the misnomer with as
much speed and tact as possible, redressing the bal-
ance with a sweet smile for the victim and a venom-
ous glance at myself.

The illustrations I could offer of this kind are so
numerous that it is difficult to choose from among
them. However, one particular instance I remember
taking place in the foyer of the little Opera House in
Monte Carlo. It must have been, I suppose, after one
of my concerts, which in that sociable spot are never
left unadorned by some party to send the musician
happily off to bed however poorly he may have
played.

There was a milling crowd of overdressed people of both sexes—by which I don't mean overcov-
ered but rather underdraped—the women with large
expanses of flesh leaving a splendid field for jewel-
lery and men in dinner jackets made of every imag-
inable material from plum-coloured plush to Turkey
carpet (circa 1910).

Diana, with our youngest son Jeremy in tow,
had become separated from me—a most dangerous
situation socially—and I suddenly espied a smallish
man with a shock of white hair, a brown face, and

alert black eyes. Darting forward, for fear he would be engulfed before I could nab him, I seized him by the shoulders, embraced him on either cheek, exclaiming delightedly: "Chagall! *Chèr Marc, comment ça va?*"

The expression of blank surprise on the face of the assaulted man totally failed to deflect my joy and I continued in much the same vein, asking him what new work he was doing (oils or watercolour?), and it wasn't until my hands—possibly more perceptive than my eyes or mind—registering the thick, furry white flannel of his jacket (the poor fellow was still imprisoned in my grip) that I sensed dimly that something was awry.

Releasing my captive uneasily, I turned to find Diana at my elbow and muttered to her, "Chagall, darling," in a kind of dying fall. She, of course, had taken in the utter stranger at one glance—ghastly "who's for tennis" jacket, black satin propeller of a black tie, velvet shoes and all—and placed him somewhere halfway down the list of Greek ship-owners without whose drachmas the tower blocks and gambling temples of that once exquisite little town would have tumbled into the sea. Offering an apology with her second-best smile, she extricated me from my predicament, adding that, especially after a concert, my faculties were dimmer than usual and that, in order to protect herself, she usually greeted me backstage with a kiss and the reminder that she was my second wife—a position that she had by then stoutly maintained for some thirty years or so.

With true Greek courtesy, the utter stranger told me that he considered I had bestowed upon him a great compliment and that he was indeed often mistaken for Chagall. I turned triumphantly toward Diana and was discomfited by a veiled glare tinged with desperation. "Well," she said, "at least you didn't mistake him for Indira Gandhi."

# Arthur Miller

**PLAYWRIGHT**

It seemed to me I had been invited repeatedly for
years to accept the ———— award given in the name
of a fine critic and an old friend of mine, T.F., dead
these twelve or fifteen years. His widow, Dora, as I
shall call her, at last prevailed, and I agreed to drive
up to a luncheon some two hours from my house, to
at last receive the honor. I have always avoided such
ceremonies.

When I arrived in the dining hall of the school,
I was surprised by the number of guests, at least two
hundred, who, I learned, had gathered for the sole
purpose of witnessing my elevation. And there coming toward me out of the crowd was the critic's wife,
whom I had not seen in almost a decade, and whose
name had totally vanished from my mind.

Nevertheless, we talked on and on about my old
friend, her deceased husband—the pleasant even-
ings we had spent together, my admiration for his
work and his learning, and the long reach of his
wonderfully balanced point of view. And as we in-
voked his memory and I could see more and more
clearly the size of his body, the outlines of his profile
and gold-rimmed glasses, the vest and jacket he
never removed, I gradually realized that I could not
recall his name, neither his first nor his last.

And so I listened to her as she spoke of him and
his affection for me, knowing that if only she would
drop a hint, a nickname, the least breath of sound
that would tip me off, I could quickly fill in the rest.
The fact was I had liked him very much and I
liked her.

Everyone was now taking seats and settling in for a pleasant hour and a half of chicken followed by the prize. Unfortunately, I was seated at one side of the podium and Dora on the other, so we found it hard to converse. There was no possibility of groping any further. The lady on my left loved the theatre, she said, but had never read "his" reviews, she having been only in high school during his critical reign. I simply could not frame a question in a way that would elicit the name of him who, in effect, we had assembled to honor through this prize.

I tried to invoke a Zenlike relaxation, a transcendancy over the happy hum of conversation; I tried pressing down hard with my heel on my instep, I pressed a fork into my palm; but neither release nor tension helped. I studied the menu, scanning it for some clue, looked for an initialed pin on Dora's dress, tried to summon up the deceased as he opened his front door to greet me—nothing I could do offered the least clue.

And now dear Dora was standing at the podium. I was sure she would have to mention her husband's name. Instead, she referred to him as "my husband." And how he had admired my work. And what he had written about my plays. Everything but his name.

Applause. I was on my feet, waiting for a silence which I hoped would be a long time coming. How to frame a speech of gratitude without offering insult and yet never mention the name of the man in whose name it was given? The applause was dying away. I grew frantic. Out of the corner of my eye I saw the glint of a large silver bowl on the table at Dora's elbow. Could this be my award? Was I losing consciousness or did I see engraving on it?

Silence in the audience. Interested faces of ladies expecting a warm speech of gratitude and praise. I walked over to Dora, picked up the bowl and turned it admiringly. "What a bowl!" I exclaimed, to cover the moment, and a ripple of uncomprehending giggling swept across the audience.

I put the bowl down and to my horror found myself planting a kiss on Dora's cheek while she half leaped up in her chair in surprise. But my dear old friend's name was engraved in the silver, and I returned to the podium and noodled on about him and his dear wife, both of whom, in all truth, had provided many an interesting evening of talk in those bygone years. And to tell the truth, I have never been happier to see a bowl in my life.

# Nigel Nicolson

BRITISH AUTHOR AND PUBLISHER

Early in 1940 I was a 2nd Lieutenant in the Grena-
dier Guards, stationed at Wellington Barracks, and
was ordered to take forty men as reinforcements to
the battalions in France. It was a simple job. I was to
march them to Waterloo Station, entrain them for
Dover, cross the Channel, deliver them to somewhere like Arras, and then return.

The war had scarcely started. There was no
fighting in France, no bombing of London. But it was
my first independent command, and I marched off
my little detachment with inflated juvenile pride.
We were accompanied by a small section of the regi-
mental band, and one or two people cheered.

We crossed Westminster Bridge. On the far side
I marked the entrance to Waterloo Station. "Left
wheel!" I cried. The columns responded. We passed
under the great portal into the courtyard beyond
which I expected to find the waiting train. There was
no sign of it, nor of any locomotive activity whatever. Instead, tall office buildings enclosed us on all
sides. A typist looked out of a window, then a dozen
or more, tittering, and a few guardsmen risked a
wave or two in response. The band faltered.

It was not Waterloo. It was the courtyard of the
London County Council. The exit on the far side was
barricaded, and there was no room for a U-turn.
"About turn!" I commanded. While this manoeuvre
was possible, and indeed smartly executed, it left me
and the band at the wrong end. We scurried round.

Then the second disaster occurred. I tripped on
the curb; fell into a puddle; and rose drenched, filthy,

and diminished. Cries of derisive encouragement volleyed from the now crowded windows. My men were kinder. I signalled to the band that any musical accompaniment to a retreat would be inappropriate. We marched to Waterloo in total silence.

# David Niven

**ACTOR**

When I was a very impecunious young officer in the Regular Army, aged nineteen (long before I became an actor and perhaps could have carried it off), I was invited to a Fancy Dress Ball at a *very* smart house in Leicestershire.

I took a lot of trouble and went as a clown, complete with pompoms, a bladder, a string of evil-smelling sausages, and a very long false nose.

I arrived early, eager to meet the immensely smart and important people I knew would be there. Few cars were about when I showed up and the butler looked a little surprised, but anyway he opened the drawing-room door and announced me. Lots of smart and important people were indeed there, and they were all in full evening dress.

I had got the right date but the wrong month.

The host and hostess insisted that I stay for dinner, and I spent a miserable night in my grease-paint seated between two dowagers who never spoke to me and beneath the pitying eyes of butler and footman.

# Michael Noakes
**ARTIST**

I had been commissioned to paint a portrait of the newly appointed Chief of Defence Staff. Since there was to be a domestic background in the picture, the first two sittings were to be held in his home rather than in my studio.

I arrived and laid out my equipment happily, and we tried out his chair in various positions in different lights. My first error was when, trying to be helpful, I attempted to pass his Field Marshal's baton to him (delicate gold filigree top, velvet-covered, presented to him by the Queen just two weeks before). Somehow I missed—and it dropped with an echoing thwang into a tin wastepaper bin. That, not surprisingly, did not go down very well.

Determined to prove that painters are not really clumsy idiots, I set to work—deliberately painting with deft, rhythmic arm movements. But I knew, as that fully loaded brush sprang out of my hand and hurtled like a rocket across his drawing room, that it was going to touch down on the one bit of the Aubusson carpet, in the far corner, that I had not protected with dust-sheets . . . and Alizarin Crimson, just right for painting the ribbon of the Order of the Bath, is unfortunately so powerful a colour that it is virtually impossible to remove the stain completely.

We had to stop for twenty minutes whilst I did what I could to put right the damage with my turpentine and his detergent. Before starting again, I asked if I might wash my hands. The Field Marshal was obviously only too glad to be rid of me for a bit and directed me to the little cloakroom by the front door.

As I washed my hands, though, I became aware that the loo was making the strangest noises. I went across to have a look at it, and, incapable of action, I watched as the water level gurgled over the brim and several gallons were deposited all over the floor.

The next time I had a sitting at the Field Marshal's home, I was filled with good resolutions as I drove up to the front door. He, looking slightly strained, I thought, greeted me there. He was, though, still surprisingly courteous: holding the door wide open for me as I carried my portable easel through, he gave me a weak smile. "Good morning, Field Marshal!" I beamed as I eased past him in a caricature of extreme care. Then the collapsible leg on the easel fell open and removed a large chunk of the door. The painting came out rather well, though.

# Rudolf Nureyev

**BALLET DANCER**

It was the last day of my holiday and I was standing on the deck of a yacht in the harbour of Piraeus outside Athens. We had just had our last bathe. There was some delay about going ashore, and I suddenly decided to have one more farewell dip. I flung off my dressing gown and jumped over the side. As I hit the water I realized that I had already taken off my wet bathing trunks. It was OK while I was in the water, but a bit more difficult when I had to climb back aboard the boat. But nobody seemed to mind.

# *Joyce Carol Oates*
**AUTHOR**

The most "embarrassing" episode of recent years took place when I was giving a lecture at Princeton and was interrupted by a distraught-looking woman in a long black coat who claimed that she and the audience had come to hear "Joyce Carol Oates," and not me. . . . For some seconds I was nonplussed: the issue of identity is always rather problematic, especially for novelists who have cultivated a number of alternative personalities. Then I apologized and explained that I had thought I *was* "Joyce Carol Oates," but perhaps I was mistaken. The woman eventually left the auditorium without further incident, but the episode left me bemused for some days.

# Tip O'Neill

**SPEAKER OF THE HOUSE OF REPRESENTATIVES**

Back in 1976 I was on my way to California to do some campaigning for my colleagues in the U.S. House of Representatives. I was on a small plane, and we had to stop in Denver for refueling.

I was stretching my legs in the terminal, and a young man came up to me and said: "Hi, Tip, how are you?" We talked for a few minutes, then he said: "You don't know who I am, do you?" Well, I had to admit that I didn't, then proceeded to explain that I meet a lot of people in my business and it was impossible for me to remember all of them. Also, that I'm easy to recognize because of my size, white hair, big nose, and the fact that I'm in the news and on TV a lot.

He smiled and said he understood. Then he explained that we had been guests at the same dinner party in Washington two weeks earlier. I was indeed embarrassed when he told me his name—especially after my carrying on about *my* name and face being so well known. The young man was *ROBERT REDFORD!*

# Norman Vincent Peale

**CLERGYMAN AND AUTHOR**

As the speaker at the annual dinner of an Eastern State Bankers Association, I arrived an hour late, went to my room, and changed into a tuxedo. Thus attired, I descended the elevator to find that all the bankers had gone into the dining hall, save one stray banker whom I encountered in the elevator. He was pretty well intoxicated.

He fixed a watery eye on me and looked me over speculatively. Apparently he did not recognize me dressed as I was, for he said in an intimate fashion, "Hello there, buddy." This was not the form of address to which I was usually accustomed, but I answered in kind, and for a moment there ensued a conversation which might roughly be described as jocular. Finally, becoming a bit more intimate, he asked, "Where are you going tonight, buddy?"

"To the Bankers Association dinner," I replied. "Where are you going?" With a look of ill-concealed disgust, he said he guessed he would have to go there also, but he added, "I don't want to, for it won't be any good."

"Why," I asked, "won't it be any good?"

"Oh," he replied, "they've got some preacher from New York to speak tonight."

"You don't mean it!" I exclaimed. "How come they have a preacher to speak to a Bankers Association?"

"You've got me, buddy, unless they've run out of money."

"Well," I sighed, "I guess we might as well go

in there anyway. There's nothing else to do around here."

"I guess I will too, but," he reiterated, "I'm telling you, it won't be any good."

"Brother," I responded, "I *know* it won't be any good."

Having agreed that the speech wouldn't be "any good" and having gotten that settled to our mutual satisfaction, he went his way and I went mine. Proceeding to the head table, I took my seat and forgot all about my erstwhile inebriated friend, until, when I arose to speak, by some sinister quirk of fate the first eye I caught at the rear of the ballroom was this man's. It was evident that he was what you might call reasonably embarrassed, for he threw up his hands in a gesture of dismay and sank down out of sight.

Finally coming up for air, he listened to my talk. When I finished, I was standing at the head table shaking hands with such persons as came forward to greet me, when I saw him coming off from the left. I could see that he hated to come up to speak to me, but I liked him, and he proved to be a dead-game sport. For, getting up in front of me, he grabbed my hand and said, "Buddy, we were both right, weren't we?"

# Gregory Peck

**ACTOR**

Several years ago on a fine morning in June, my wife and I were languishing in the garden of our house on Cap Ferrat. The last thing we wanted to do was to leave the premises. We received a phone call from David Niven, inviting us to lunch at his villa, a lunch to be given that day for Prince Rainier and Princess Grace, their family, and various members of European royalty who were in Monaco for the wedding of Princess Caroline. The group was to come to David's directly from a rehearsal of the wedding. The lunch was to be very informal . . . come-as-you-are . . . and all was to be relaxed and joyous with absolutely no publicity. I said no thanks. In a while a handwritten note from David was delivered to our front door, importuning us to come. Again, all was to be easy and enjoyable; we would love it, etc., etc. We gave in.

When we arrived at David's villa, Lo Scoglietto, the first thing we saw was a mob of fifty or more paparazzi darting around the house and climbing the walls. We fought our way inside. We had dressed as David had suggested, slacks, shirt, halter, nothing to speak of. We made our way into the garden where the party was in progress. Everyone else was soberly dressed. No one introduced us to anyone. David skittered about nervously, avoiding us, we thought. We struck out on our own, and presently I found myself in conversation with a handsome European lady of a certain age. I had no idea who she was. We talked about travel, of Switzerland, of Portugal, the United States. I fished around for her station in life but couldn't make it out. Finally, she ventured the information that her son now lived in Madrid. I seized on this lead. "Do you visit him often in Madrid?" "Oh, yes," she said. "Often, now that he is King."

The following night, at the prenuptial ball, we were properly attired . . . my wife beautiful in a splendid St. Laurent, me in white tie and tails. The palace was packed with fashionable people, important jewels and full decorations on display. There were several orchestras playing in various parts of the palace, and champagne bars were everywhere. I fell to chatting with a fellow who looked vaguely familiar. He told me that he had not seen me since we were filming *The Guns of Navarone* on the Isle of Rhodes in 1960. Desperately I searched my mind for his identity. Remembering that there was an outdoor café scene in the film in which we used several hundred local residents as extras, I said, "Oh then, you must have been in the café scene." I must say he was a good sport about it . . . he did smile faintly as he said, "No. I am Michael of Rumania."

# Frank Perdue

**CHICKEN MOGUL**

I have a bad habit of writing a speech I'm supposed to give about an hour before it's to be presented. Leaving LaGuardia on the shuttle to speak in Boston, I was preoccupied with the contents of the speech. I worked on the material throughout the whole flight. The speech was ready just as the flight attendant announced we'd be landing in Washington in a few minutes.

# Norman Plastow

**ARCHITECT**

I worked for several years with a Hungarian woman architect whose command of the English language made one realize how versatile and subtle it can be. One of her best efforts occurred at a meeting where a scheme for an old people's home was being discussed. The discussion was brought to an abrupt halt by her profound observation: "A woman is as old as a man feels her, but a man is as old as he feels himself."

# André Previn

## COMPOSER AND CONDUCTOR

The process of adopting a Vietnamese orphan is, quite correctly, fraught with difficulties. My family has now been graced by these children three times, but I still remember one slightly insane moment during the first adoption attempt. Visiting my house, prior to the final sanction, was a remarkable lady named Rosemary Taylor, who had led a selfless existence in Saigon, running an orphanage. I doubt whether I will ever meet anyone more suited to eventual sainthood than this extraordinary woman. She was a weekend guest in my house in Surrey, and, needless to say, we underestimated her sense of humour and her sense of the occasion, and bent over backward to make everything with which she came into contact seem to spring from the pages of an ideal-home magazine.

Now, at the time, my small sons were addicted to an admixture of health-food cereals, which they consumed with gusto each morning. I personally thought it vile, but they loved it, and I presume it was good for them. The stuff was kept in one of several large glass containers in the kitchen. On her first morning in my house, Miss Taylor appeared for breakfast. She asked for cereal, and I gave her a large bowlful, lauding the energy-giving qualities of this blameless concoction. She poured milk over it, disdained the use of sugar, and fell to. She ate in silent contemplation, and if there was any dissatisfaction on her face, I missed it. Finally, the bowl empty, she pushed it away. "I have to be honest with you," she said, "I'm not really crazy about it." My eyes happened to glance at the various glass jars around the cupboard. A realization hit me. I blanched. Finally, I managed an answer: "Actually, I'm not surprised," I said as gently as possible. "I've just made you eat a large dish of hamster food."

# Ronald Reagan

**PRESIDENT OF THE UNITED STATES**

During my early days in radio broadcasting, I was a sports announcer for WHO in Des Moines, Iowa. Since we were not a large station, many of us had to do a variety of jobs. A well-known evangelist from Los Angeles came to Des Moines to hold a series of revival meetings, and I was asked to interview her. From baseball and track to Aimee Semple McPherson just about stretched my versatility to its ultimate limits! The interview went smoothly; Miss McPherson was very gracious, and she made an eloquent plea for the success of her meetings. Suddenly I heard her say good night to the audience, and I was sitting there with four minutes to fill. Since I didn't know enough about Aimee Semple McPherson to fill in that time, I signaled to the engineer to play a record. Then, in a very dignified tone, I informed the audience that we would conclude the broadcast by the noted evangelist with a brief interlude of transcribed music. Of course, I expected nothing less fitting for the occasion than the "Ave Maria." What our sleepy engineer grabbed off the record stack, and played for a doubtlessly astonished audience, was the Mills Brothers singing "Minnie the Moocher's Wedding Day!" I can't tell you how grateful I was that the radio audience couldn't see this announcer's red face!

# Mary Renault
**AUTHOR**

While an undergraduate at Oxford, I used to go to read in the British Museum reading room. Looking up from my book, I was often fascinated by the eccentric-looking elderly ladies at neighbouring desks. After letting my imagination play on them for some time, I wrote a piece for the college magazine called "Witches at the Museum." Shortly after it appeared, I was sent for by the principal. It seemed that the people I had described, far from having, as I supposed, emerged from obscure bed-sitters, were eminent scholars from other universities. I had described them so vividly that she recognized them all. Since I had depicted them engaged in sorcery, vampirism of infants, and similar pursuits, and was informed that some of them took the magazine, this interview comes fairly high in my embarrassment scale.

# Frank Reynolds
## NEWS CORRESPONDENT

Several years ago I was interviewing a Governor from a midwestern state. He was a candidate for reelection and was not expected to win. (He didn't.) During the interview he went on at some length about the joys of campaigning, getting out and meeting the people, etc. It was well known to reporters that he detested that sort of thing, so I asked him for a few examples of how great it was to be on the stump, shaking hands and kissing babies. He couldn't think of anything right away, so he began talking about how the campaign had allowed him to spend more time with his wife, because they traveled around the state together and attended all the same meetings and rallies. To my horror, I then heard myself say, on live television, "Well, politics, as they say, really does make strange bedfellows."

The Governor turned green. I prayed that an earthquake might occur, but both of us gamely flailed on till the end of the broadcast. The only redeeming factor was that most people were watching a football game on that autumn afternoon. Never have I been more thankful to have been on a program with a mercifully small audience.

# Sir Ralph Richardson

**ACTOR**

During the war I was given special leave from the Navy to make a film about submarines. We were shooting in a submarine lying in Liverpool Docks. On the way back to our hotel after the day's activity, the late Charles Victor and I shared a taxi to the Adelphi Hotel. Charles was heavily made up with full beard and dressed as a naval officer. I was more or less playing myself and in civilian clothes. We were just about to get into the lift at the hotel when the manager approached me and expressed his pleasure and gratification that I was patronizing his august establishment.

"You will let me know," he urged, "if there's anything at all we can do to make your stay comfortable."

"A bottle of wine?" I suggested.

"We'll have it sent up to your room immediately."

By this time Victor was growing a little impatient. He was manifestly not to be included in the celebrations. The manager accompanied us into the lift and pressed the button for the sixth floor.

"If it's not too much trouble," said Victor, "I would like to get out at the floor below."

The manager reluctantly halted the lift, and Charles got out.

"Do you know, sir, who that was?" the manager said to me, and before I could reply, he continued, "That was the actor Ralph Richardson."

Who he imagined I was remains one of the great unsolved mysteries of the Second World War.

# Diana Rigg
**ACTRESS**

I was in my dressing room at the Old Vic, changing after a performance of *Jumpers* and chatting to my mother, when there was a knock at the door. The visitor turned out to be Albert Finney, who was rehearsing *Hamlet,* the next production in the theatre. My mother, anxious to prove herself in the theatrical swim, turned to Albert Finney, enquiring brightly, "And when are you going to give us your Hammy?"

# Gene Roddenberry

**WRITER AND PRODUCER**

My greatest gaffe, and a peculiarly embarrassing one, came in Huntsville, Alabama, in 1979, when I was addressing a group of college students, professors, and space scientists on the subject of "A Science-Fiction Writer's Look at the Future." In that talk, as part of making a certain point, I compared the difference between nuclear *fission* and nuclear *fusion*. My words got the two of them "bassackwards" which, to the brains in that audience, would be like referring to water as "carbon dioxide." During the question period, a gray-haired and scholarly gentleman from the audience called this gaffe to my attention. All I could do was turn red and mumble my appreciation.

# A. L. Rowse

**HISTORIAN**

I still blush to remember the worst gaffe I ever made, though it was years ago and I had an accomplice in my crime.

It happened in the garden of the niece of the famous Mrs. Keppel, the beautiful friend of King Edward VII. I had arrived for the weekend while my hostess was away visiting a neighbouring country house. Tea was brought in to me in the library, and I was comfortably enjoying crumpets when I had the misfortune to look out of the window. To my horror, I saw that a young bullock had broken into the garden and was busily engaged in rooting up a young sapling in the drive.

I called in the butler, and together we sallied forth to get the animal out through the gate at the bottom. That butler was no countryman but a townie. While I tried to drive the reluctant young steer down the drive, the fatuous man held the gate open in such a way that the whole herd of cattle came pouring in to join their companion inside the garden! And with all our efforts, we could not get them out again.

You should have seen the shambles they made of that beautiful garden, which had been all tidied up and put in apple-pie order for the weekend. Those young miscreants, a score of them, knew perfectly well what they were up to; they had been longing to get through the fence and into that paradise for weeks.

They went down on their knees to root at the other saplings, putting their heads and incipient horns to the young trees—I can see them now. They trampled the rose-beds; they bit off whatever they fancied; they rolled in the dirt. Those bullocks were just like a band of naughty boys who had been waiting to do all the mischief they could inside the prohibited garden. And we simply could *not* get them to go back down the drive and out through the gate! At every effort we made with one group, another would break away and make for another area to damage. Of course, the cattleman, the only person who knew how to handle them, was away for the afternoon. Even the butler gave up and went indoors. I waited disconsolately until their keeper came back and got them all out.

The spectacle of desolation they left behind them was a scene I shall never forget. I have never been invited to that house again for the weekend. And I don't wonder.

# Charles M. Schulz
### CARTOONIST

When I was at Sanford Junior High in St. Paul, Minnesota, we were instructed to read a certain novel and, naturally, prepare a written report over Christmas vacation. Such assignments have always disturbed me, and I still do not understand a teacher destroying the Christmas holidays in this manner.

At any rate, I failed to read the book and, naturally, had no report ready for when school began the Monday after the holidays. I went to school that morning with a terrible dread, but was taken quickly off the hook with the news that our teacher had slipped on the ice and broken her arm. This is one of my fondest memories of school days.

# Gaia Servadio

AUTHOR AND JOURNALIST

I had been promised one of those things which make journalists happy and which could rightfully be regarded as a sign of acute masochism by those outside the trade: to be granted a special visa for a visit to the car factory at Togliattigrad on the Volga. In fact, I must say right away that the visa never materialized, since the Soviet factory, which had been provided by Fiat, was running into disastrous delays and was not ready. However, as I was in Turin, I asked to see the Mirafiori factory, and at the end of my visit I was given a superb little model of a Fiat 128 (I think, I am never sure about models).

Back home, my son coveted this perfect little car and so I gave it to him: it became his favourite toy. But on one of my visits to his room, which was in a state of chaos, I promised him that if he did not put it in order, I would throw everything out of the window. On the following day the room was chaotic, and I kept my promise. How could I do otherwise? Mothers must keep their word. But Owen was miserable: the one toy he really cared for had fallen four floors and was in pieces. So I suggested that he should write to Gianni Agnelli, since he had stayed at his house, and, after all, he was Fiat's chairman. Owen wrote. I didn't see the letter, and some time went by.

A few weeks later a telephone call came from British Fiat, and the manager was on the line. "The car is ready," he said, "but won't some spare parts do instead? At Bradford we can make it as good as new."

"No," I said, "it is really smashed up."

"Which colour do you require?"

"Mine was blue, but it doesn't actually matter —any colour will do," said I.

Slightly embarrassed but very kindly, he enquired how it had fallen and from what height.

"Well, it was from the fourth floor, from my son's bedroom window."

There was another pause. "But can you tell me how it came to fall from there?"

Embarrassed, too, I had to confess that I myself had thrown it out.

Visualizing the person with whom he was talking as a mighty strong woman with the muscles of a Hercules, he remained silent until, unfortunately, I added that it had been my son's favourite toy.

A model of the car arrived on the following day.

# William Shatner

ACTOR

You can only be embarrassed in front of people that you know or care about. If you do something idiotic in front of strangers, at least you can laugh it off and say, "They didn't notice," or, "Who cares." But when you know them and like them, admire them and seek their appreciation, and then do something —that is embarrassing.

I was invited, some years ago, to a summer lunch at Josh Logan's country home. The hoi polloi of American Theatre were there, but how was I to know? The invitation from Josh, for whom I was working at the time, was merely, "Come for lunch." It said nothing of wearing summer tux or silken gown. To my complete consternation, when I arrived in my jeans and T-shirt, that is what the hoi polloi were wearing. I had my young daughter in one hand and a half-grown Doberman pup in the other. When I say puppy, please get the picture of an eighty-pound ruffian.

As I looked across the manicured lawn of Josh Logan's beautiful country estate and saw Merle Oberon, Henry Fonda, Gloria Vanderbilt, and many others of that ilk, my first impulse was to turn and run. My second impulse was to drop the baby and run. On my third impulse, which was to run after the puppy who had gotten loose and had flung himself into the swimming pool, I acted. I yanked the dog out of the pool, dropping the baby to the ground in the process, not knowing at that moment where my values lay. And then the dog, glistening with water, took one look around at the many beautifully dressed people and selected the ever-lovely, ever-beautiful, and completely-enclosed-in-white Gloria Vanderbilt. Running up to her, he jumped up with his muddy paws, and two long brown streaks appeared on the front of her dress. Not completely satisfied with that, he proceeded to shake himself dry, using the long white chiffon gown as a towel. At that moment I was ready to trade the baby for a train ride home. Everybody saw my embarrassment and tried to cover it, and the rest of the afternoon stretched on.

Years later, I met Henry Fonda on an airplane, and, thinking as we all do that the incident was long-since forgotten by everyone but the embarrassed person, I said, "Mr. Fonda, I don't suppose you remember me. . . . " but before I could get the rest of the sentence out he said: "Aren't you the actor who was at Logan's party and whose dog dirtied Gloria Vanderbilt's dress?" I was even more embarrassed the second time. In fact, I don't think I have ever truly apologized until this moment. Dear Gloria, I hope you knew a good dry cleaner.

# Sidney Sheldon
**WRITER**

A few years ago I acquired a lovely blue Rolls-Royce. I went shopping in Beverly Hills and parked in front of a shop on Rodeo Drive. I went inside, did my shopping, returned to my car, and got behind the driver's seat of the Rolls. An arm reached through the window and grabbed my shoulder, and a voice said, "What do you think you're doing?" I looked out the window, and there stood an enormous Texan. "This is my car," he said. "No, it isn't," I told him. It's mine." To prove it, I started to put the key in the ignition, and it didn't fit. I realized what had happened. I said to him, "I'm terribly sorry, but I'm driving the same model and color Rolls and I obviously parked right in back of you." And as he stood there watching me, I got out of the car and walked in back—to my wife's white Volkswagen, which I was driving that morning.

The second incident involves a screenwriter named Helen Deutsch, who wrote many of MGM's top movies. Helen took a trip to New York and while there had a hat made for her at Lilly Daché. It was a beautiful creation with feathers and frills, and she was assured that it was the only one of its kind. She went to lunch at Twenty-One, and at a table across the room was a woman wearing the identical hat. The woman looked at Helen, and Helen, being a good sport, smiled and shook her head as if to say, "I guess we were both fooled, but it doesn't matter." The woman turned to her escort, and they both looked at Helen. Sure that they had obviously misunderstood her meaning, Helen pointed to her own hat and then to the woman's hat and nodded and smiled. The man at the table called over the captain, and the three of them were staring at her. Deeply embarrassed, Helen made one more effort to clarify the situation. She pointed to her hat, then at the woman's hat, shrugged and gave them a big smile. The captain called over the maître d', and there were now four of them staring at her. Lunch was forgotten. Helen called for her check and slunk past the table, out of the restaurant. As she passed the mirror in the reception room, she saw that she was not wearing her new hat.

# Beverly Sills
**COLORATURA SOPRANO**

When I was just starting out on my singing career, I had a great friend in Brooklyn whose mother was an avid fan of my singing. In fact, she was such a fan that she asked me if, upon her death, I would come to the funeral and sing "Ah, Sweet Mystery of Life." I agreed. And it was even written into "Aunt" Hazel's will.

Several years later, I went off on a concert tour. When I arrived in New York and walked in the front door, the phone rang. It was Hazel's daughter.

"Beverly, Aunt Hazel died. The funeral is this afternoon. Will you come and sing, as you promised?"

"Oh," says I distractedly, "I can't. I have to leave for a concert in Albany. Gosh, I wish you'd given me a few weeks' notice. . . . "

Needless to say, that was the last I ever heard from *that* friend.

# Neil Simon
**PLAYWRIGHT**

One day while having lunch at the commissary of Paramount Pictures, I was seated with Walter Matthau. We were busily chatting when Roman Polanski came over to our table to say hello. He was then beginning work on *Rosemary's Baby* but had just received worldwide acclaim for his thriller, *Repulsion.* We were in the midst of conversation when I spotted, out of the corner of my eye, a friend who was obviously headed for our table to say hello. I knew introductions were in order, but I could not for the life of me remember this fellow's name. Then, the instant he arrived at our table, it hit me. Sidney! But the rest of my brain was in a dither. I looked up and said, "Oh, hello, Sidney. You know Walter, and this, of course, is Roman Repulski." Quick as a flash, Walter tried to remedy things. He said, "Roman recently directed *Polansian.*" The rest of lunch was uneventful.

# Andrew Sinclair

**NOVELIST AND BIOGRAPHER**

A friend of mine from Australia was asked to an elegant party in Eaton Square. Caviar was to be served after the champagne. Having drunk too much of that, my friend found his way to the bathroom. He groped around for a light switch but did not discover it. He then groped around for a lavatory but did not discover one. Finally, he found the edge of the bath and settled for that. He relieved himself slowly and fully, then turned on the taps to swill away the evidence.

   Going back to the party, he asked his hostess where the caviar might be. "Packed on ice," she said, "in the bath. I am just going to get it." He went instead, walking quickly back to Australia.

# B. F. Skinner

BEHAVIORAL PSYCHOLOGIST

I once enjoyed a buffet supper with a group of students. I was sitting in a dark corner when the hostess, who was Chinese, brought me a plate. She pointed to a dark brown paté of some sort and made a comment which I did not understand. I attacked it with knife and fork. It had a wonderful crispy crust, and I wondered how the Chinese were able to get that effect so beautifully. I cut into it and put some in my mouth, again admiring the culinary skill of my hostess as I chewed. Then I noticed that the young woman sitting beside me was peeling the same object on her plate. This Chinese delicacy was a hard-boiled egg.

# Sally Struthers

**ACTRESS**

I turn a color quite close to crimson when I remember this one. My friend, "Miss Judy" I call her, and I strolled into a posh Beverly Hills restaurant one afternoon for a smart lunch. She and I established a signal years before so that if she sees someone she knows by name, but can't remember it, she is to say in an ever-so-perky voice, "Hi, there!" That's my cue to follow with, "Oh, hi, Bob," or, "Oh, hello, Mrs. Torkildsen." Miss Judy can always count on me to supply the person's name. (I'm good with names. Never forget a face.) Well, this particular day I entered the restaurant walking behind Miss Judy. I heard her say in the special voice, "Hi, there," and I peeked around from behind her (she's also referred to by some as "Big Judy") to supply the name. When I saw the gentleman she had greeted, I also said, "Hi, there," and sat down confused and embarrassed. I *knew* I should know him, and he was sitting at a table across the restaurant, smiling at me and obviously waiting for me to come over. I couldn't go over. I did not know his name. I furtively signaled the maître d' and asked him to please check the reservation book and let me know the name of the man sitting at the first table by the door. I prayed the reservation would be in *his* name, rather than the name of the fellow he was lunching with. A few moments later the maître d' returned and whispered the mystery man's name in my ear. Miss Judy said, "Well . . . who is it?" Stunned, I replied guiltily, "It's only the person who's been making five percent of my income for the last eight years. It's my business manager!"

# Terry-Thomas

**ACTOR AND COMEDIAN**

I was fifteen and on summer holidays in Coombe Martin, and very ambitiously invited two girls and their very severe mother to tea in a grotto café in Lynmouth.

Having rehearsed the ordering of the tea, I was able to converse with the waitress in a lordly manner. I then relaxed for a few seconds, beaming with satisfaction at my impressed guests. Suddenly something clicked and I realized I had forgotten a vital ingredient. "Waitress," I called, "I nearly forgot to order my very favourites—please add some Lemon Turd Carts."

# Abigail Van Buren

ADVICE COLUMNIST

I was booked a year in advance to address a national convention of builders in Palm Springs, California.

My secretary had been out ill and did not remind me of the speaking date, although she had accepted it and it was in her file.

I was introduced and an entire audience waited for me to appear. Of course, I didn't show.

When I was advised of this gaffe, I wrote to apologize and offered to attend their next convention at my own expense and speak gratis to prove my sincerity. Exactly a year later, they took me up on it.

# Joseph Wambaugh
**WRITER**

In 1971, while still a member of the Los Angeles Police Department, and being hailed as a new and unique publishing oddity (cop-turned-best-selling-author), I decided to help publicize my first novel, *The New Centurions*. Several other authors, including Irving Stone, were also on promotional tours at the time. One afternoon while I was being interviewed by three newspaper reporters in a hotel bar, a woman wearing a conventioneer's name tag rushed among us breathlessly, waving an autograph book.

"Is The Author here?" she cried.

And I, aglow with my new celebrity, and from cocktails at noon, obligingly produced my signature pen.

Alas, she looked confused and disappointed. *"You're* not Irving Stone!" she accused.

Indignant, I puffed and sputtered for an instant, but quickly rallied. "No, madam," I sneered. "I'm Truman Capote."

With just a hint of malice, she smiled and said: "I declare, Mr. Capote, I'd never have recognized you. On television you're so much more *masculine."*

# Dame Rebecca West
**AUTHOR**

Years ago in Washington a lift stopped and then shot up with only a nice-looking lady and myself. We were both guests at a big dinner. I looked at her and said pathetically, "Do tell me who you are." And she said, "Well, I am Mrs. Truman, but I often wonder."

I am bound to say that her smile was so sweet that I might have been giving her a bouquet rather than dropping a brick.

# Mrs. R. Wheller

My daughter Nicola works at Technical College and has been deeply involved with the organization of a comparatively new department. Recently she had occasion to show an inspection committee over the new unit.

"How do you feel, Miss Wheller," asked one member, "now that you've got this project off the ground?"

"Actually," said my daughter, "I'm exhausted after only two days into the course."

A shocked look spread over the face of her questioner. "I beg your pardon?" he said.

"I'm exhausted," repeated my daughter, "and we're only two days into the course."

"Oh, I see." He looked relieved. "I thought you said after two days' intercourse."

# E. B. White

**AUTHOR**

Many years ago, before I had learned the ways of hospitals, I showed up one morning at St. Luke's in New York for an X ray of the gastrointestinal tract, one of my least favorite tracts. I had a briefcase under my arm when the nurse guided me into a small, dimly lit dressing booth across the hall from the X-ray room. My hearing was evidently not as sharp as it might have been, for I understood her to say, "Take off all your clothes except your shoes and socks, and (pointing as I thought to the briefcase) put that down there (indicating a little seat in the booth). The X-ray room is across the hall, and you will be called when they are ready for you."

I dutifully took off all my clothes except my shoes and socks and waited, unaware that the nurse had said, " . . . and put on that gown there." (I hadn't seen any gown, but there must have been one, lurking in the gloom.)

When my name was called, I thought, Well, if this is the way they do it, it's all right with me. And I strode boldly forth, looking as silly as any man does in just shoes and socks. I recall whistling softly to keep my courage up. In the hall I encountered nobody, but when I entered the X-ray room—a large, drafty place—the nurse screamed. "No, no, no!" she cried. "Put your *gown* on!" And she led me back and pointed to a miserable little garment hiding under my briefcase. It was an embarrassing moment, but on the whole a merry one. I've often thought of it.

# William Whitelaw

**MEMBER OF PARLIAMENT**

I was attending a reception at the American Embassy several years ago and was introduced to an American whom I did not know. After I had spoken to him for some time, I went to a friend and said, "Do tell me, who is that American I was talking to about golf? He doesn't appear to have much sense of humour." My friend replied: "Bob Hope."

# Herman Wouk

**WRITER**

Shortly after Neil Armstrong returned from the moon, he and I happened to be at a large weekend gathering. I wandered into a bar where several of my friends were standing around, glasses in hand. "Ah," said the astronaut's host. "Here's Herman Wouk. Herman, you know Bill here, and Sam, and Harry— and of course you know Neil." I looked blankly at the most celebrated man on earth—it was not a bright bar, and I was not in bright form—and I said, "Neil Who?" Ever since, in that little company, I have been known as Herman Who. Armstrong, to round out the story, couldn't have been more gracious as I was sinking through the floor in apology.